# RAILWAYS

CHRISTIAN WOLMAR is an author and broadcaster specializing in transport matters. He writes regularly for national newspapers and the specialist press. His many books include *The Subterranean Railway*; the bestselling *Fire and Steam: How the Railways Transformed Britain*; *Railways and the Raj*; *To the Edge of the World*; and (for Head of Zeus) *The Story of Crossrail*.

# THE LANDMARK LIBRARY
*Chapters in the History of Civilization*

The Landmark Library is a record of the achievements of humankind from the late Stone Age to the present day. Each volume in the series is devoted to a crucial theme in the history of civilization, and offers a concise and authoritative text accompanied by a generous complement of images. Contributing authors to The Landmark Library are chosen for their ability to combine scholarship with a flair for communicating their specialist knowledge to a wider, non-specialist readership.

ALREADY PUBLISHED

*The French Revolution*, David Andress
*Guernica*, James Attlee
*City of Light: The Reinvention of Paris*, Rupert Christiansen
*Shakespeare: The Theatre of Our World*, Peter Conrad
*Skyscraper*, Dan Cruickshank
*Hadrian's Wall*, Adrian Goldsworthy
*The British Museum*, James Hamilton
*Eroica: The First Great Romantic Symphony*, James Hamilton-Paterson
*Versailles*, Colin Jones
*Magna Carta*, Dan Jones
*Messiah*, Jonathan Keates
*The Arab Conquests*, Justin Marozzi
*The Rite of Spring*, Gillian Moore
*Stonehenge*, Francis Pryor
*The Sarpedon Krater*, Nigel Spivey
*The Royal Society*, Adrian Tinniswood
*Voyagers*, Nicholas Thomas
*Dante's Divine Comedy*, Ian Thomson
*Olympia*, Robin Waterfield
*Railways*, Christian Wolmar

FORTHCOMING TITLES

*Escorial*, John Adamson

# RAILWAYS

CHRISTIAN WOLMAR

HEAD
of ZEUS

*An Apollo Book*

First published in the UK in 2019 by Head of Zeus Ltd
This paperback edition first published in the UK in 2022
by Head of Zeus Ltd, part of Bloomsbury Publishing Plc

1 3 5 7 9 10 8 6 4 2

A CIP catalogue record for this book is available from
the British Library.

ISBN (PB)  9781788549851
ISBN (E)  9781788549837

Designed by Isambard Thomas

Printed and bound in Great Britain by
CPI Group (UK) Ltd, Croydon CRO 4YY

FSC
www.fsc.org

MIX
Paper | Supporting
responsible forestry
FSC® C171272

Head of Zeus Ltd
5–8 Hardwick Street
London EC1R 4RG

WWW.HEADOFZEUS.COM

*Previous pages*
Hal Morey, *Grand Central Station, c.1929*

*Chapter openers*
Homage to A.M. Cassandre's *Étoile du Nord*

Picture Credits
p. 4–5 Getty Images; p.15 UIG / IMechE / akg-images; pp.22–3
Hulton Archive / Stringer / Getty Images; pp.26–7 Universal
History Archive / Getty Images; pp.32–3 Hulton Archive /
Getty Images; pp.36–7 Pictures From History / akg-images;
p.40 Science & Society Picture Library / Getty Images; pp.44–5
World History Archive / akg-images; pp.52–3 Heritage Images /
Getty Images; p.54 Bridgeman Images; p.57 Sheridan Libraries /
Getty Images; p.64 The Stapleton Collection / Bridgeman
Images; pp.72–3 Hulton Archive / Getty Images pp.74–5
Science & Society Picture Library / Getty Images; pp.78–9
Science & Society Picture Library / Getty Images; p.85 Science
& Society Picture Library / Getty Images; pp.90–1 Hulton
Deutsch / Getty Images; p.93 Public Domain; pp.94–5 Library
of Congress / Getty Images; pp.100–1 Universal History
Archive / Getty Images; pp.102–3 Otto Herschan Collection /
Springer / Getty Images; pp.108–9 Universal Images Group /
Getty Images; pp.118–9 Buyenlarge / Getty Images; pp.132–3
Science Source / akg-images; pp.138–9 Roger Viollet / Getty
Images; pp.140–1 Oxford Science Archive /akg-images;
pp.146–7 Public Domain; pp.156–7 Illustrated Papers Collection
/ Bridgeman Images; pp.158–9 Science & Society Picture
Library / Getty Images; p.161 Heritage Images / The Print
Collector / akg-images; p.164 Peter Newark American Pictures
/ Bridgeman Images; p.167 Pictures From History / Bridgeman
Images; p.168 Archives Charmet / Bridgeman Images; p.169
Keystone France / Getty Images; p.175 Science & Society
Picture Library / Getty Images; pp.182–3; Chicago History
Museum / Getty Images;  pp.186–7 Universal Images Group /
Universal History Archive / akg-images; p.188 Heritage Images
/ Keystone-Archive / akg-images; p.191 Pictures From History /
akg-images; pp.196–7 Central Press / Stringer / Getty images;
p.198 Public Domain; pp.202–3 Public Domain

# Why Railways?

No one person invented the railways. It was a joint effort by many people, most of whom are long forgotten and consequently nameless, as it took centuries for the various components that make up a railway system to be developed and brought into use. It was only when all these various inventions could be brought together that the age of the iron road could begin.

Leaving aside the wheel, whose origins stretch back as far as 4,500 BC, and the chariot, which probably first appeared around 2,000 BC, there were three key developments: the concept of making tracks to bear a carriage's wheels in order to reduce resistance, the invention of steam engines, and then, the Eureka moment, combining the two.

Putting down wooden planks to ease the progress of carts or wagons was a practice that stretched back to long before the birth of Christ. It has been suggested that it was used by the ancient Greeks to drag boats across the isthmus at Corinth (where the canal was not hewn out of the rock until the end of the nineteenth century). A stained glass window in the Minster of Freiburg im Breisgau in southwestern Germany, dating back to 1350, depicts wagons that appear to be running on rails. There is also evidence that crude tracks were used to haul wagons up the steep slopes of Hohensalzburg Fortress in the Austrian city of Salzburg in the early sixteenth century.

In England, during the first decade of the seventeenth century, a mining engineer called Huntingdon Beaumont – a name that seems to come straight out of a Jane Austen novel – went much further by laying 2 miles (3.2 km) of track linking a pit belonging to Sir Francis Willoughby in Nottinghamshire to the River Trent. That was to be the pattern for the vast majority of what came to be known as 'wagonways', whose principal purpose was to take coal, and sometimes other minerals, from pits to the nearest river or, later, to canals, and thence to the coast, from where the cargo could be taken long distances by sea. Transport was the main determinant of the price of coal and reducing its cost was therefore the key stimulus behind the development of these wagonways and, later, the early railways.

It was not in England's East Midlands, however, but in the northeast, with its vast number of pits, that these wagonways spread rapidly from around the mid-seventeenth century. The wagons were, of course, pushed or pulled on the tracks by men or horses and sometimes simply by gravity if there were an incline for them to roll down. This was not always safe. Indeed, what could be called the first railway fatality occurred in 1650 when two boys were, according to a contemporary report, 'slain with a wagon' on a wooden wagonway at Whickham in County Durham.

These early 'railways' were not cheap to build and one report suggests a cost of £785 per mile for a track laid in 1726. While comparisons with today's money are tendentious, a reasonable estimate would be around £1m a mile in today's money, which means it was a considerable amount for a mine owner. However, the tracks could increase the productivity of the wagon drivers fivefold, as well as making the transport less dependent on the weather. (Rain rapidly turned the dirt roads of the time into quagmires.) By greatly reducing the cost of producing coal, the tracks ensured that mines became more profitable. By the end of the seventeenth century, they were so widespread in the northeast that they were known as 'Newcastle Roads', but later the term 'tramway' became commonplace.

Maintenance of the tracks was also a considerable expense. The wood on which the wheels travelled invariably wore out within a couple of years and this quickly led to iron being used for the rails, initially as an overlay on the wood, but by the second half of the seventeenth century, the idea of rails made entirely of iron had been mooted. By the beginning of the nineteenth century, there was an extensive network of tramways, some of which were interconnected as the owners of the pits formed consortiums to merge lines. On occasion, however, rivalries led owners to ban their neighbours from crossing their land or to charge exorbitant 'wayleaves' for permission to do so.

Conservative estimates of the extent of these wagonways nationally put it at 133 miles (214 km) by 1750 and just under 300 miles (483 km) by the end of the century. Their growth thereafter was rapid, Tyneside alone boasting 225 miles (362 km) by 1820. These early nineteenth-century tracks were crude and lightly constructed. Most of them used flanged tracks which had a lip to prevent derailments and consequently enabled ordinary wagons with the right axle width to use them without adaptation. Later, as more sophisticated wagons were developed for use solely on rails, the flange was shifted from rail to wheel, where it remains to this day.

Steam engines for use on the tracks were also developed over a long period of time. As with tracks and wheels, the origins of steam power stretch back to antiquity. The Roman writer and civil engineer Vitruvius, writing in the first century BC, mentions a device called an aeolipile, comprising a ball spun by steam jets. While this was a bit of nonsense with no constructive purpose, it was the first recorded attempt to harness steam power. Various patents for steam power were taken out during the seventeenth century in Europe and Arabia but the first prototype of what became a steam engine was developed in 1663 by Edward, Marquis of Worcester, who produced a sort of pump that used a cooling system to create the vacuum that is the basis of steam power. A Frenchman, Thomas Savery, produced a similar device but the real breakthrough was made by Thomas Newcomen, an ironmaster from Devon, who around 1705 built the first device using a piston inside a cylinder, the key to all future steam engines. Making use of a recently invented, improved version of smelting iron, he built machines that were able to pump water from mines. His invention helped to keep the tin and copper ore industry viable as his pumps were able to draw water from mines that could no longer be worked because of flooding, and put them back into production. The installation of his pumps quickly spread and by 1733, when his patent expired, there were more than fifty, and possibly 100, in operation.

The other great innovator was James Watt, who, during the final third of the eighteenth century, made a series of refinements to Newcomen's engines, greatly enhancing their efficiency, and adapting them for a wide variety of uses. Boulton & Watt, the business he created in 1775 with Matthew Boulton, a manufacturer from Birmingham, became the world's leading builder of steam engines. Thanks to a series of patents, the company gained a monopoly on all steam engine development to the end of the century. The steam age was born and Watt was undoubtedly its midwife. The scale of the Industrial Revolution he helped trigger can be gauged by the fact that there were 30,000 steam-powered looms in Manchester alone in the mid-1820s when plans for the Liverpool & Manchester Railway, the first to rely entirely on steam power, were first set out.

Boulton & Watt had provided the engine for the first successful steam-powered boat, the *Charlotte Dundas*, but combining steam power with wheels to produce locomotives was a far trickier task because of the heavy weight of the equipment needed to produce and make use of the steam. In the final third of the eighteenth century, there had been various attempts to create a self-propelled wheeled vehicle powered by steam engine, starting with Nicholas Cugnot's *fardier à vapeur*, which made its inaugural and only run in Paris in 1769. Unfortunately, it hit a wall and overturned and was consequently declared a *danger publique*, but it still gets fond mentions in motor-car histories as the first powered and wheeled device to operate on a road.

While other attempts were made to run steam engines on

roads, most of them failed to get off the drawing board and there are few challenges to the claim that Richard Trevithick, a Cornishman, was the 'father' of the railway steam locomotive. His ground-breaking innovation was to use high-pressure steam that gave a better power-to-weight ratio than the low pressure that was the basis of the Boulton & Watt engines. In 1801 his road carriage, nicknamed the *Puffing Devil*, was able to travel a short distance under its own steam, but Trevithick had failed to devise a proper steering mechanism and the vehicle plunged into a ditch. Worse, Trevithick and his friends, having decided to drown their sorrows in a local hostelry, forgot to douse the fire under the boiler, which promptly exploded. Undeterred, Trevithick built an improved engine and sensibly put it on rails, thereby getting round the problem of steering. The use of iron also enabled a significant improvement in rail technology and in 1803 Trevithick's engine hauled a set of wagons weighing 9 tons at an impressive 5 mph (8 km/h) at Pen-y-Darren ironworks in south Wales. While this is reckoned to be a world first in terms of steam engine haulage, the weight was still too great and the locomotive was soon converted to a stationary engine which used cables to haul the wagons.

It was another five years before Trevithick produced his final and most famous effort, the locomotive playfully called *Catch Me Who Can*, which he demonstrated on a circular track in Bloomsbury just south of the present location of Euston station in London. It was announced with a fanfare and lots of hype, and Trevithick promised odds of 10,000 to one if 'any mare, horse or gelding' could outpace his engine. The train and tracks were presented to the public in the summer of 1808 as Trevithick's 'Steam Circus' and were hidden behind a high fence, so the curious had to fork out a couple of pennies even to get a glimpse of the new-fangled device. The braver ones who dared to ride on the train, which reached speeds of up to 15 mph (24 km/h) on a

Richard Trevithick's 'portable' steam engine *Catch Me Who Can* ran on a circular track near the present site of Euston station for several weeks in the summer of 1808 carrying passengers who had to buy a ticket like the one shown here.

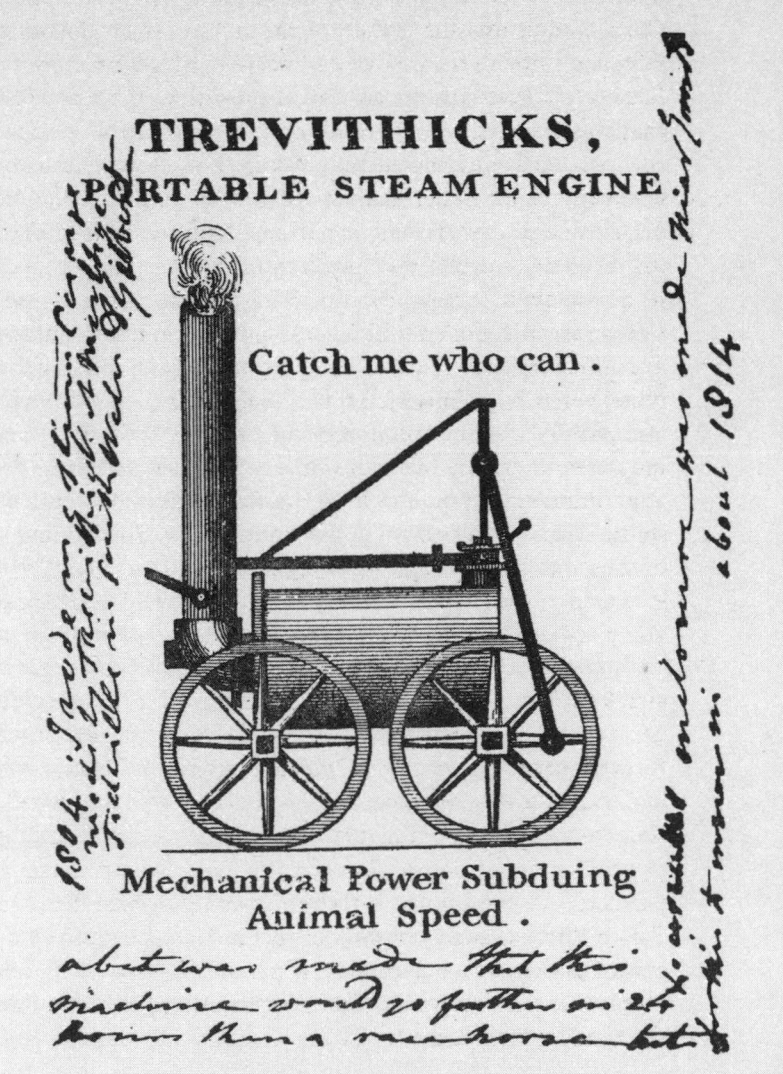

THE LOCOMOTIVE OF 1808.

From Harper's 'A Cornish Giant.'

FIG. 5.

good day, had to pay another shilling (5p, equivalent to around £5 today). The venture lasted for a couple of months but interest had already started to wane even before the line's closure after the rails – yet again – proved insufficiently strong to support the locomotive, leading to a break and a derailment. As for Trevithick's challenge to quadrupeds, no race between horse and engine was ever run, so the inventor did not have to pay out. Trevithick went bankrupt the following year nonetheless, and left England to seek his fortune in distant Peru as a mining consultant. He returned but died in 1833, broke and long forgotten.

Trevithick's legacy, though, was crucial. Others, notably George Stephenson, would pick up the baton. While no innovator himself, Stephenson was adept at improving and adapting other people's inventions, a talent that has earned him, slightly erroneously, the reputation of being 'father of the railways'. Born in 1781 in Wylam, 8 miles (13 km) west of Newcastle, in a house that directly abutted the local mine's wagonway, Stephenson started life as a brakesman in that colliery, a duty which required overseeing the pump and winding wheel mechanism for hauling the coal up from the pit. In his spare time, he would work at ways of improving the various machines that were being introduced to facilitate the extraction of coal. Stephenson developed a reputation as a repairman, capable of bringing broken-down machinery back to life, and his interest soon turned to steam locomotives. He went to see the operation of the Leeds & Middleton Colliery line, a wagonway that had first operated in 1758 and which, in 1812, had just become the first railway to use steam locomotion commercially.

Its locomotive, designed at the instigation of John Blenkinsop, the Middleton colliery manager, and based on Trevithick's *Catch Me Who Can*, was revolutionary in two other ways: it used a rack-and-pinion system to cope with the steep incline; and rather than having only a single cylinder – as had been the case with all previous engines – its engine had two cylinders, which provided a far more balanced thrust. Stephenson was greatly impressed and within a couple of years had produced his first engine, *Blücher*, named after the Prussian general who had led the army fighting alongside the British at Waterloo, for use at the Killingworth colliery in Durham where he had been appointed engine-wright. The tracks from the mine involved a steep incline but Stephenson's engine successfully hauled eight loaded coal wagons weighing 30 tons at a speed of 4 miles (6.4 km) an hour. He went on to develop several more locomotives for Killingworth, and subsequently for the nearby Hetton colliery line near Sunderland.

Several other pioneers were active in producing locomotives at this time, but some colliery owners and other promoters of railway lines continued to believe that the tried and tested method of using horses to haul wagons was the cheapest and most efficient. Stephenson, however, remained adamant that they were wrong and never deviated from his conviction that steam locomotives, and not horse power, represented the future for railways. But all these early locomotives remained primitive, frequently breaking down, putting almost unsustainably heavy loads on the tracks, and losing steam through every join. Nevertheless, the loads they carried were increasing rapidly, transforming the economics of both the coal and transport industries. In 1822 Stephenson completed an 8-mile (12.9-km) line linking the Hetton mine with the River Wear and his 'iron horses' were used on the flat sections where they were able to haul a remarkable load of 64 tons.

...

By the mid-1820s both locomotives and railway tracks were beginning to be a proven technology and the idea that the development of the railways could have a major impact on society was beginning to be understood. In one respect, the railways were lucky, in that other potential technologies, which might have made alternative methods of transport more efficient, had either not been developed yet or were found wanting. There is quite a long catalogue here. First, the tarmac surface which is now universal even on lightly used roads was only just emerging. Roads had begun to be upgraded in the late eighteenth and early nineteenth centuries by pioneers such as Thomas Telford and, particularly, John McAdam, who developed the concept of binding small pebbles with stone dust to create a smooth surface. Thanks to McAdam's techniques and the transfer of responsibility for maintenance from local parishes to the Turnpike trusts, which had been set up by Parliament to collect tolls to finance the upkeep of the principal roads in Britain, many main roads were improved radically. Journeys by stagecoach, the only available form of long-distance travel, became faster and smoother. Nevertheless, the surface of the roads still cracked in severe weather conditions and ruts and potholes invariably slowed down the traffic. Average speeds were 12 mph (19.3 km/h) at best: the fastest stagecoach service of the time, the London–Shrewsbury 'Wonder', in 1835 boasted of a service that covered the 153-mile (246.2-km) journey in thirteen hours. As Stuart Hylton, the author of a history of the early railways, remarks, this was 'scarcely better than the record for the distance travelled overland in a single day by the Roman Emperor Tiberius': he had covered 200 miles (322 km) using relays of horses and chariots.[1]

Away from the main roads, at the time the first railways were being developed and, indeed, throughout much of the nineteenth century, the condition of the vast majority of roads remained atrocious, little more than rutted paths that could barely take the weight of a coach and horses. They were certainly not up to coping with a heavy steam engine, although this did not deter some brave inventors from trying out the idea of running locomotives on them. They were hampered, however, by legislation which greatly constrained road use. The turnpike owners – rightly wary of the damage that such vehicles might do – imposed prohibitive tolls, sometimes up to fifteen times that for a horse and cart. Then, just as the technology was improving and the roads becoming more stable, making the concept feasible, in 1865 the government passed the Locomotive Act, known popularly as the Red Flag Act, which limited speeds to 4 mph (6.4 km/h) in rural areas and just 2 mph (3.2 km/h) in towns where, to the ignominy of the drivers, a man waving a red flag had to walk 60 yards (54.9 m) ahead in order to warn the townspeople of the approach of a self-propelled vehicle; given the noise the engines made, this was a clearly unnecessary but onerous restriction.

As well as the absence of a network of paved roads, another key invention not available at the time of the development of the first railways was the pneumatic tyre. This was a crucial requirement in making road transport more economic and enabling a far smoother ride for vehicles. The internal combustion engine was also an invention of the late nineteenth century and it is not fanciful to suggest that, had these breakthroughs been made earlier, they might well have stymied the development, or at least the rapid spread, of the railways. Steam power required such a large weight-to-power ratio that it was never likely to be able to be deployed on roads; it is the low level of friction between steel wheels and iron (or steel) rails that is critical to the railways' efficiency.

The railways arrived at a time when the need for transport – and not just of coal – was beginning to increase. The latent demand for travel across the country can be illustrated by the extensive use of stagecoaches. By 1835, there were around 4,000 stagecoaches hurtling round the country, carrying 10 million passengers per year. However, there was little potential for growth. The volume of traffic on the roads had increased, causing both congestion and damage to the surfaces, and there were fundamental problems with the use of horses, as some of the early railways which experimented with them found to their detriment. The cost of feed had risen rapidly after 1820 because of the rise in demand; and the need for the stagecoach companies to run frequent fast services led to a decrease in the horses' life expectancy, adding further to running costs. The experience of the stagecoach operators showed the railway companies that such a large number of horses would have been required to provide services on a long stretch of track that the idea was unfeasible. Locomotives were the only viable alternative.

The railways not only superseded the stagecoaches, but also later effectively put paid to the canals. The network of canals that had first emerged in the second half of the eighteenth century expanded rapidly in the fifty years or so before the advent of the railways. By 1820, the United Kingdom had just over 100 navigable canals, with a total length of around 2,700 miles (4,345 km). However, horse-hauled barges were slow and, while more suited than the roads of the era for carrying heavy minerals or aggregates, they were of limited use to passengers. There were some passenger barges on a few short-distance routes but long-distance journeys were clearly out of the question. This was not merely because of the length of time they would have taken, but because there was no national network of canals – rather, a haphazard collection of waterways with differences in widths and lock sizes and a complex ownership pattern, resulting in an arbitrary system of tolls that made it too expensive to run profitable services.

Railway technology also enjoyed the advantage of being further developed than any of its potential rivals, and the economic imperative of reducing the cost of coal was a crucial factor in its continued enhancement. All this pointed to the railways as an invention whose time had come. They had everything going for them and the success of the first railway lines would give further impetus to technical progress. The coming of the railways also captured the imagination of the public, whose enthusiasm would help the railway companies to acquire the capital they so desperately needed for future development.

In fact, the railways had an almost unquenchable thirst for capital investment. The symbiotic relationship between the railways and economic growth, however, is difficult to unravel. The minds of many great economists have dwelled on the chicken-and-egg nature of the issue, but all agree that the two go hand in hand. Railways stimulated economic growth, but then also expanded relentlessly and rapidly themselves because of the nation's increasing affluence, an affluence that they had actually helped to bring about. Once the railways appeared, the economy began to grow more quickly wherever its tentacles spread around the country, allowing the fruits of the Industrial Revolution to be shared more widely. This economic growth in turn helped fulfil the key requirement for the creation of railways, the availability of capital. Early promoters struggled to find backers but, as the success of the railways became evident and industry boomed, capital became available from a wider range of investors and a burgeoning middle class seeking potentially profitable ventures in which to put their money.

It was invariably local business interests that supported the promotion of the first lines. Not only did they have a direct commercial incentive but they were also often the only source of capital. There are fierce disputes among railway historians over what was Britain's, and indeed the world's, first major railway, but the claims of the Liverpool & Manchester, which opened in September 1830, cannot realistically be challenged. Since the turn of the century, there had been numerous lines that were pioneering in one sense or another, but none had the characteristics of a modern railway. They were basic affairs whose principal function was to carry coal or other minerals, mostly to a waterway.

OVERLEAF The 5-mile-long Swansea & Mumbles Railway was the first in the world to carry passengers. It opened in 1807 and was horse drawn until 1896, after an experiment with a sail failed. Later run by electricity, it closed in 1960.

These precursors, nevertheless, created the conditions necessary for the Liverpool & Manchester's birth. For example, there was the 9-mile-long (14.5-km-long) Surrey Iron Railway, incorporated in 1801, and opened two years later, which ran between Wandsworth and Croydon and has claims to be the first line open to anyone prepared to pay the toll. This was a horse-hauled railway used to carry minerals and agricultural produce in this heavily industrialized area around the River Wandle. It was later extended further out to Godstone and Merstham, but plans to create a 50-mile-long (80-km-long) line to Portsmouth never materialized.

The Surrey Iron Railway carried only freight and it is the Swansea & Mumbles Railway that is widely recognized as the first for passengers. The main purpose of the 5-mile (8-km) line, opened in 1806, was to connect the city's docks with the mines and quarries at Mumbles, at the western end of Swansea Bay. It was operated by horses and, in another world first, occasionally by sails. One of the original shareholders, Benjamin French, had the novel idea of offering rides to passengers and bought the rights to do so for a mere £20. Trips in his coaches started the following year, at a cost of a shilling (5p, or around £5 in today's values) and the railway thrived. Remarkably, it did not replace its horses with steam engines until the 1870s.

These are the lines that were, at least, successful enough to be remembered and recorded. There were countless other attempts to develop railway technology or to operate services but they lie long forgotten as they failed at an early stage or were simply abandoned. These efforts were important in that they proved various aspects of the technology and whetted the appetite of the public for train travel, but they also demonstrated that it was worthwhile investing capital to provide infrastructure that could be used for many years. Capitalism was in its infancy and such schemes were instrumental in demonstrating its potential.

The apogee of the wagonway was the Stockton & Darlington Railway, in which George Stephenson played a crucial role. The line was conceived as a solution to the perennial problem of how to get coal to a waterway as cheaply as possible. However, it was Edward Pease, a local Quaker and woollen manufacturer based in Darlington who was, along with his son Joseph, the driving force behind its promotion. Stockton was a port but the river that served it, the Tees, was unsuitable for navigation. Darlington was the main town in the area, with a population of over 5,000, and had become prosperous as a centre for the local textile industry. An initial plan to build a canal between the two was strongly opposed locally, but the first plan for a railway was defeated in Parliament. The older Pease, who also had banking interests, persisted and a second bill was passed, thanks to the large amount of capital which he contributed both directly and through persuading his fellow local Quakers to support the scheme.

Enter George Stephenson. The original route approved by Parliament had been drawn up by George Overton, a Welsh engineer, and Pease appointed Stephenson to produce a new alignment. He managed to knock 3 miles (4.8 km) off the original scheme and then, assuming a much wider role in the line's development, made a series of decisions that would have a lasting impact on the development of the railways. These included establishing the 4 foot 8½- inch gauge, using wrought iron for the rails and insisting, against much advice to the contrary, on steam traction. In fact, since the line was open to any user who paid the fee and local businesses invariably did not have access to steam engines, most of the 'trains' were horse-hauled. Stephenson also made several mistakes: he used very short lengths of rail, which made for a bumpy ride, and eschewed the wooden sleepers that had become prevalent on wagonways; instead, he chose rigid stone sleepers, which would be the cause of a large number of rail breaks.

OVERLEAF George Stephenson's *Rocket* hauling a train in 1925 to mark the 100th anniversary of its first journey between Stockton and Darlington.

The small local builders charged with constructing the Stockton & Darlington faced some challenging natural obstacles: notably Myers Flat, an area of marshland, and the River Skerne, which had to be crossed. But the work passed off relatively smoothly, taking just three years. The official opening of the Stockton & Darlington on 27 September 1825 attracted considerable interest, even from abroad, principally because it was the world's first public railway to operate steam engines. The large crowds who attended the inaugural ceremony also witnessed an unofficial race between local horsemen and the 'iron horse'. It was Stephenson himself, whose enduring fame is testimony to his skills as a self-publicist, who drove his locomotive, *Locomotion*, along the line, on occasion reaching the dizzy heights of 15 mph (24 km/h) while hauling an 80-ton load of coal and flour in six wagons as well as twenty passenger wagons. He easily outpaced the riders and covered the 12 miles (19.3 km) between Darlington and Stockton in three hours, including several stops.

In truth, though, the much-fêted railway was a ramshackle affair with few of the attributes of a modern railway. The line was mainly used to carry coal from Darlington to Stockton. Only freight was steam-hauled: passenger trains were horse-drawn and had just one coach. Passenger traffic was light, since the railway served a series of villages and mines rather than major towns. Worst of all, the single track resulted in chaotic operating conditions. Trains travelling in opposite directions met frequently as there was no signalling system. Arguments and sometimes fist fights erupted over who should reverse to one of the rare passing loops. The situation was exacerbated by the fact that there was no one in overall control. In a move that fitted the free market *zeitgeist* of the early nineteenth century, the directors of the Stockton & Darlington had decided that they would not run their own trains but, rather, allow anyone who wanted to use the tracks to transport goods or people. The chaos created by this free-for-all proved to be instructive for future railway promoters who realized that they had to retain control of their asset by running the trains themselves and providing the traction to do so. The lessons of the Stockton & Darlington were quickly learnt. Creating an integrated system with trains and track both operated by the same company would be the pattern of nearly all future railways for the next century and a half, disrupted only by the late-twentieth-century move towards privatization and what is now called 'open access' which is intended to allow rival operators to run on the same tracks.

The centenary of the Stockton & Darlington was celebrated in 1925 and British Railways made huge efforts in 1975 to mark its 150th anniversary, suggesting it was the world's first railway, but in reality it was instead the last of the wagonways. Its inadequacy means that the accolade of being the world's first railway really has to go to the Liverpool & Manchester, completed in 1830, although others, notably in the US, quickly followed suit.

# The Idea Takes Root

The Liverpool & Manchester Railway was on a different scale from the Stockton & Darlington. Its creation was, like that of its predecessor, stimulated by local business interests, but its very name, showing that it linked two major towns (soon to become cities and now boasting world-famous football clubs) demonstrates that it was a far more substantial enterprise than the strictly non-league Stockton & Darlington.

The Industrial Revolution, with its origins in the north of England in the eighteenth century, had seen both Manchester and Liverpool grow rapidly through coal and iron production. Lancashire was, in fact, that era's 'Silicon Valley', industrialization and mechanization growing faster there than anywhere else in the world. The rapidly expanding port of Liverpool carried 80 per cent of the cotton imported into Britain, some 1,120 bags daily, and Manchester had become a hive of manufacturing activity with an estimated 30,000 steam-powered looms by 1824.

This was, therefore, natural and fertile territory for an innovation such as the Liverpool & Manchester Railway which was steam-hauled, double-tracked, carried both freight and passengers, and ran between two major conurbations. The inadequacy of the existing transport system was the principal stimulus for its creation. Trade between the two towns amounted to 1,000 tons per day, but goods were carried on the inadequate local roads: 'The scene was that of a daily flow of hundreds of pack-horses, farm cars, lumbering horse-drawn wagons and stage coaches. Coach journeys between the two towns took four or five hours, including stops to change horses.'[1] Accidents were frequent and winter weather at times prevented traffic from

The Liverpool & Manchester, which opened in 1830, had a variety of carriages for passengers. Shown here are first-class carriages drawn by the locomotive *Jupiter*, and second-and third-class carriages drawn by the locomotive *North Star*.

getting through. Nor were the canals, which had expanded in the area since the opening of the Mersey & Irwell Navigation in 1750, up to the task. Although they handled much of the freight traffic, their functioning was affected by the vagaries of the seasons – high winds and frozen surfaces in winter, and shallow water in summer – while 'their slow and circuitous routes through the quiet countryside'[2] made theft of their cargoes a year-round threat.

It was the Liverpool traders, rather than the Manchester industrialists, who were keenest to harness the new technology. The initial driving force was Joseph Sandars, a Liverpool corn merchant and, importantly, a Parliamentary reformer with good political contacts. As early as 1821 he had had a meeting with William James, a colliery owner and builder of wagonways, paid him £300 to conduct a survey for the railway, and formed a committee to further the scheme. Inevitably, the proposal for a railway was subject to objections from the canal owners. Hunter Davies, in his biography of George Stephenson, suggests rather wittily that it was their gentlemanly conduct of the project that created difficulties: 'All the Liverpool promoters were reasonable, solid, well respected citizens and one of the earliest moves they made, when their committee was formed in 1822, was to inform the canal people of their plans and grievances, suggesting to the Bridgewater [the main canal between the two towns] trustees that they should reduce their exorbitant rates.'[3] The trustees steadfastly refused to reduce what were, effectively, monopoly prices. Davies reckons the canal owners could have delayed the construction of the railway by a decade had they been more amenable to change. Instead, after being rebuffed, Sandars and his committee pressed ahead.

When George Stephenson, invited by Sandars, appeared on the scene in 1824 to take over the survey work, the canal owners did start to reduce their rates but it was too little, too late. With continuing developments in engine technology and the imperative for improved transport between the two towns becoming stronger daily, the advantages of a railway were now all too apparent.

As Stephenson set about his work, he discovered that not everyone was keen on the idea of a railway and that opposition was well organized. In a letter to his former employer in Darlington he wrote: 'The ground is blockaded on every side to prevent us getting on with the survey. Lord Sefton [one of the canal owners] says he will have a hundred men against us.'[4] Fights broke out frequently, surveyors were stoned and leaflets playing on local people's fears widely distributed. It took Stephenson and his team four months to complete the necessary survey, but the scheme then foundered in Parliament as the bill to enable its construction was rejected in May 1825 – after no fewer than thirty-seven committee sessions. Poor Stephenson was ill-equipped to act as advocate for the scheme in front of aristocratic MPs and their clever lawyers, and his lack of preparation and precision was exposed. There were, too, technical errors in his presentation as he had delegated too much work to inexperienced junior assistants, one of whom was so consumed by anxiety that he committed suicide in Stephenson's office.

Stephenson was sacked, but then recalled after a second bill was successfully steered through Parliament in May 1826. It was recognized that his skills in designing and organizing the construction of a railway were second to none. The work, which started almost immediately, was undertaken by hundreds of navvies, specialist railway construction men named after their predecessors – navigators – who had carved out Britain's canals. Stephenson was everywhere and did everything: he selected people for the key jobs, notably Thomas Gooch, his secretary and draughtsman who would go on to be the company's civil engineer until 1844, and trained them himself. He 'sketched rough plans

OVERLEAF The canals were largely put out of business by the advent of the railways. This engraving shows 'Barges on the Bridgewater Canal', from *The Illustrated London News*, 18 October 1851.

for bridges, level-crossings, cuttings, embankments, machinery, turntables and track, and Gooch translated them into working drawings ... in the absence of appropriate tools, and equipment, Stephenson had to design some of his own. He often chalked a rough outline on a piece of wood or the workshop floor.'[5]

Stephenson had understood the need to produce a route that was appropriate for a railway, without sharp curves or steep inclines. His line therefore followed the natural contours of the hills, but where possible ran straight. The task was far from easy, since there were numerous rivers and streams to be crossed. The seemingly bottomless peat bog of Chat Moss, which presented a 5-mile-long (8-km-long) barrier to the railway and was 30 feet (9.1 m) deep in parts, appeared almost unbridgeable. At times, both men and horses were obliged to don sections of flat wooden planks, rather like skis, in order to work on this treacherous terrain. Whatever material Stephenson's team dumped into the bog simply disappeared, and it seemed that no viable route for the railway would be found across it. The directors of the company became increasingly concerned; progress was painfully slow and the venture was costing far more than they had bargained for. Eventually, despite many mishaps and near disasters when men fell into the bog and had to be rescued, Stephenson devised a system using large timbers to create a railway that 'floated' on the surface of Chat Moss. It was not until the first day of 1830 that the line across it was completed thanks to Stephenson's insistence that a stable surface should be created by sufficient piling. Samuel Smiles, who wrote the first biography of Stephenson in the second half of the nineteenth century, reveals the extreme difficulty of building a railway line across Chat Moss, describing how the 'floating' track was laid before the ground underneath was stabilized:

Several hundreds of men and boys were employed to skin the Moss all round for many thousands yards, by means of sharp spades, called by the turf cutters 'tommy-spades' and the dried cakes of turf were afterwards used to form the embankment, until at length as the stuff sank and rested upon the bottom, the bank gradually rose above the surface, and slowly advanced onwards, declining in height and consequently in weight, until it became joined to the floating road already laid.[6]

It was a triumph for Stephenson, but he had never doubted his own ability, well summed up by Hunter Davies: 'George was always confident in his powers, dismissing the cautious as weak and the critics as fools, completely convinced he would win through in the end.'[7]

If Stephenson's role in completing the survey and the track-laying were not enough, he was also responsible for the engines that were used on the line. In this enterprise, however, he received considerable assistance from his son Robert, who was a better locomotive engineer than his father. The choice of engine was decided at what became known as the Rainhill trials, held in a village east of Liverpool in October 1829, a kind of beauty contest for locomotives designed to test their effectiveness. There were, in fact, only four serious entrants to this momentous event – in addition to a joker who had put in a horse enclosed in metal and called it *Cycloped*. A crowd of an estimated 10,000 people eagerly cheered on the engines, creating an atmosphere not unlike that of a horse race meeting. In addition to the Stephensons, all the major locomotive engineers of the day had entered their best efforts, which were, under the rules, required to pull a train of 20 tons at 10 mph (16 km/h) or more along the 1.5-mile-long (2.4-km-long) track for ten return trips. Ultimately, however, none of Stephenson's rivals could put up any serious competition.

John Ericsson, a Swedish engineer, flattered to deceive in *Novelty*, reaching 28 mph (45 km/h) but his engine leaked

THE ROCKET OF MESS.RS R. STEPHENSON & C.º

*Weight 4 Tons 5 Cwt of 10 Horse power; Gained the Prize for the best Locomotive October 1829*

THE NOVELTY OF MESS.RS BRAITHWAITE & ERICSSON.

*Weight 3 Tons 18 Cwt of about 7 Horse power*

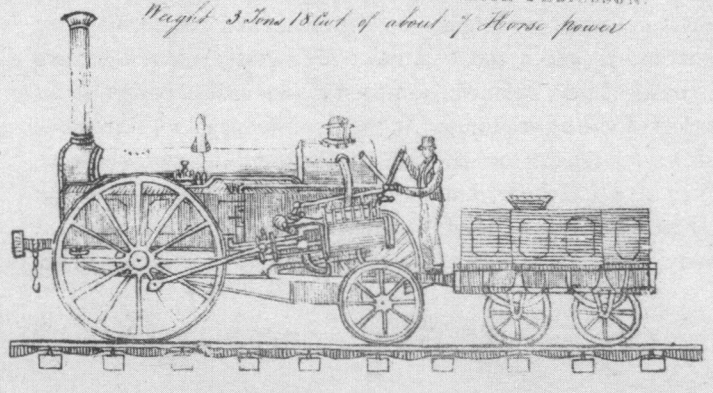

THE NORTHUMBRIAN. OF MESS.RS R. STEPHENSON & C.º

*Weight 6 Tons 3 Cwt of 14 Horse power*

badly and was disqualified; *Sans Pareil*, designed by Timothy Hackworth, who would later become a successful locomotive engineer, was found to be overweight by the judges and, in any case, Hackworth's effort spluttered to a halt in a blaze of burning coke cinders from the furnace and steam from the leaky boiler; *Perseverance*, designed by Timothy Burstall, proved to be sadly misnamed as it was quickly withdrawn when its team failed to repair damage incurred on the way to the trials.

The Stephensons, therefore, were barely challenged. Robert had cleverly devised a new type of boiler, using multiple tubes rather than just one. In combination with several other improvements, this ensured that their engine, *Rocket*, performed perfectly. It went up and down the track without fail at an average of about 14 mph (22.5 km/h) until, on the last run, Stephenson, at the controls, opened up the regulator to reach 30 mph (48 km/h). Stephenson won the £500 prize and – much more valuable to him – the contract for building all the engines for the line.

The scene was now set for the grand opening of the Liverpool & Manchester Railway, which took place nearly a year later on 15 September 1830. By then numerous tests and trials had been undertaken successfully and the plan was to run several trains from Liverpool right through to Manchester amid much pageantry and celebration. The engineering proved equal to the task and the trains' journeys were a huge success, but the event was marred by an accident that caused the first railway fatality.

The opening was attended – despite his technophobia – by the prime minister, the Duke of Wellington. When his train reached Parkside, near Newton-le-Willows, around the halfway point on the line, it stopped to take on water. Alongside other passengers, Wellington decided to wander onto the tracks to stretch his legs, where he was spotted by William Huskisson, the local MP and supporter of the railway, who had fallen out with him a couple of years earlier. Eager to make amends and possibly

Three early locomotives, 1831.

wishing to get back into the cabinet, Huskisson went over to shake Wellington's hand, but as he did so, a shout went out that a train was approaching. While most people climbed back onto the train in good time, Huskisson, who had a gammy leg, stumbled, panicked and ran to the duke's carriage, which he struggled to board because there were no steps. The unfortunate member of Parliament for Liverpool was unable to avoid being hit by the train that was being hauled by the *Rocket*, and the impact shattered his leg. Huskisson was rushed towards Manchester in a train driven by George Stephenson in the *Northumbrian*, which reached the remarkable speed of 35 mph (56 km/h), thrilling the crowds who were oblivious to the unfolding tragedy. His condition was now so grave that it was decided to stop the train in Eccles, a few miles short of Manchester. The stricken MP was taken to the local vicarage, where he was treated by doctors, but he succumbed to his injuries later that evening.

The festivities, however, continued as planned and nothing could take away from the fact that the world's first interurban railway, double-tracked and operated solely by steam locomotives, was open for business. The Liverpool & Manchester Railway was an instant success, not just in reducing the cost of freight transport between the two towns but also, significantly, in carrying passengers. Ignoring the numerous dire predictions from various prophets of doom who warned of the dangers of being unable to breathe because of the excessive speed of the locomotive and the risk from exploding boilers, which – despite the shortcomings of the early technology – proved to be a thankfully rare event, people flocked to this new form of transport. The line's reputation was helped by the musings of a young actress, Fanny Kemble, who, though just twenty-one, was rather taken by the gruff George Stephenson, with whom she claimed rather playfully to be 'horribly in love', and by his trains. Given a ride before the official opening, Kemble mused afterwards that on leaving Liverpool through the Olive Mount cutting – which still surrounds the throat of Lime Street station today – 'these great masses of stone had been cut asunder to allow our passage thus far below the surface of the earth; I felt as if no fairy tale was ever half as wonderful as what I saw. Bridges were thrown from side to side across the top of these cliffs, and the people looking down upon us then seemed like pigmies standing in the sky.'[8]

...

While the Liverpool & Manchester Railway was attracting worldwide attention, the first lines across the Atlantic were also beginning to emerge, largely using imported British technology. America, which had only just freed itself from the colonial yoke, was well behind Britain economically and industrially at this time. The development of the early rail*roads* – a term imported from Britain which Americans still use today – was stimulated by competition between the great cities of the eastern seaboard, which all sought access to the cheap agricultural produce and minerals of the midwest. Ultimately, Baltimore beat Philadelphia, Boston and New York by starting work on the Baltimore & Ohio, a line which, as the name suggests, was intended to reach the Ohio river, 280 miles (450 km) away.

The initial section of the Baltimore & Ohio railway opened in May 1830 and the first trains to run on the new line – as would be the case with several European countries – were hauled by horses. Despite clear available evidence of the viability of locomotive technology, the promoters of the railroad decided to hold a trial between horses and locomotives to establish the best method of traction. The competition was held in September 1830 and the little engine *Tom Thumb*, built locally and driven by the inventor Peter Cooper, impressed on the test run, easily covering the line's initial 13 miles (21 km) of track without stopping and reaching a top speed of 18 mph (29 km/h). The powerful grey horse competing against the engine was left well behind, but on the return trip the animal managed to coast past *Tom Thumb* as Cooper had overreached himself and snapped a pulley which brought the locomotive to a halt.

The horse's victory, however, proved pyrrhic since Cooper's engine had so impressed the railway's owners that they plumped for locomotive traction. Indeed, given the length of the proposed railway and the hilly nature of the terrain, any notion of horse traction was fanciful as far too many would have been required to enable the line to operate at a profit. Nevertheless, it would take a couple of years for locomotive haulage to become accepted as the only option. While the Baltimore & Ohio was indeed a pioneering railway, its tracks only reached their terminus at Wheeling, West Virginia, on 1 January 1853, following a series of delays caused by legal, financial and technical difficulties.

Further south, there was a far longer pioneering line, the Charleston & Hamburg, in South Carolina, which used American technology, notably the first engine built at the West Point

Peter Cooper's locomotive *Tom Thumb* lost out to the horse-drawn train in a race carried out on the Baltimore & Ohio Railroad in 1829, but nevertheless steam power was chosen for the line.

Foundry in New York, the *Best Friend of Charleston*,* on its inaugural test run in December 1830. The new railway was needed to help the local cotton industry. Like all the early lines, it was built primarily to carry freight; in this case to connect the port of Charleston with the cotton farmers inland, greatly reducing their cost of transport. The railroad's engineer was Horatio Allen, who had been to England to see the latest developments in rail technology. Like Stephenson before him, Allen brooked no argument against the use of steam traction. He recognized that the power of contemporary locomotives would soon be greatly improved, whereas the capability of horses – however well they were fed – would not. The work was arduous, especially in the summer heat and, as with most of the lines built in the South before the Civil War (1861–5), the bulk of the labour was provided by slaves bought by the railroad company. A long section of the route passed through the heavily forested Pine Barrens, which was relatively easy railway territory, but in marshy land elsewhere the rails had to be supported by timber pilings and the track was

---

* The *Best Friend of Charleston* was to suffer a tragic fate in early 1831 when an inexperienced fireman, annoyed at the sound made by the escaping steam from its safety valve, sat on the offending piece of machinery. It proved a fatal move since the boiler exploded, killing the hapless fellow, scalding the driver and reducing the engine to a hunk of scrap.

therefore elevated above the ground, a difficult engineering feat.

The 136-mile-long (219-km-long) line opened in 1833, and was, for a few years, the longest in the world. The Charleston & Hamburg (or, to give it its full name, the South Carolina Canal & Railroad Company) boasted a number of modern features, including numerous loops (which enabled trains to pass one other on the single-track line), the adoption of solely locomotive traction from the beginning and its impressive length. The fact that it ran the first steam-hauled passenger service in America suggests it was more comparable to the Liverpool & Manchester than the more famous Baltimore & Ohio. As the railway historian Stewart H. Holbrook puts it, this was a pioneering railway which was technically far more advanced than its northern contemporary: 'while the Baltimore & Ohio was fooling around with sail cars and with horse-treadmill locomotives, the Charleston & Hamburg ... had the first American-built steam locomotive'.[9]

History has rather neglected the South Carolina Canal & Railroad Company. That is partly because it was built in the South, which had many fewer foreign visitors than the North, but also because the line was soon subsumed into another company and its pioneering role forgotten, whereas the Baltimore & Ohio lived on as an independent company until the Second World War, perpetuating the idea that it was the US's first major railway line.

In one respect, the American railroads were similar to their European counterparts. After many gauges were tried, notably by railroads that wanted to keep neighbouring rivals off their territories, the US railroads settled on the same standard gauge, the 4 foot 8½ inches randomly set by Stephenson père. However, in most ways, US lines differed greatly from those on the other side of the Atlantic. They were, for a start, much longer, since America's sheer size made the distances they had to cover far greater, and they went through territory that was sparsely, if at all, populated. The locomotives that used the American railroads also presented a significant contrast, both in terms of their look and their engineering. The height and width of US locomotives was much greater than those used in Europe, not least to accommodate the huge, bulbous chimneys so characteristic of them, which were necessary to contain the sparks from wood-burning fireboxes that might otherwise set fire to the surrounding countryside. The engines were a little over 3 feet (0.9 m) taller than European ones and far more powerful, enabling them to haul heavier and longer loads. And there was another key change. Since the greater length of the journeys meant engine drivers were likely to be working very long hours, cabs were immediately introduced. In Europe, where the lines were shorter, early locomotives had no protection for the drivers.

American railroad tracks, too, were built in a different way, with the emphasis on keeping costs down. Lines were generally laid to avoid gradients, which meant following the contour lines of hills. Where inclines could not be avoided they were steeper than in Europe as US locomotives were more powerful and able to climb better. Tunnelling, which is both expensive and time-consuming, was generally avoided. For passengers, rather than the compartment style carriages that were almost universal in European trains in the nineteenth century, open-plan carriages were the norm, with access to toilets which were installed right from the start owing to the length of journeys through territory with no intermediate stations.

Both in the US and in Europe, the early lines were successful in attracting people and freight, but also, crucially, in economic terms. There were soon many imitators ready to invest in railways and governments began to realize that this was not a passing phenomenon but rather the creation of a new world. Everyone began to get the railway habit.

# Railways Everywhere

Given the technical difficulties, the need for capital and the opposition from vested interests, the spread of the railways both in Europe and in America in the first decade after the opening of the Liverpool & Manchester Railway was quite remarkable. Although much of the early investment came from private sources, there was no escaping the fact that governments had to be involved, either directly – as in the case of Belgium, where the network was designed by the government of the newly established state – or as a facilitator, as in, for example, Germany and France.

In Europe, much of the early technology came from Britain as did, more unexpectedly, many of the early locomotive drivers who learnt their trade on their domestic railways and then found that their skills were easily transferrable. The first line in France, covering the 14 miles (22.5 km) between St Étienne and Andrézieux in the Massif Central, was completed in 1827 with the aim of carrying coal from the mines to the River Loire, whence it could be transported easily to the rest of the country. Initially horse-drawn, the trains were soon operated by locomotives and the line's success led to an extension to Lyons which also became well used by passengers. The French equivalent of George Stephenson, with the same polymathic attributes, was Marc Seguin, a locomotive engineer and designer of Europe's first suspension bridge across the Rhône at Tournon in southern France. He produced the first two engines for the line and made numerous improvements to the technology, some of which found their way back to England where Robert Stephenson adopted them for his locomotives.

Despite the constraints of travel and communication at the time, the railways were a truly global enterprise with England, and the Stephensons, at their core. In Belgium, for example, at the inaugural ceremony marking the opening of the first line, George Stephenson provided the locomotives, and drove one himself after it initially broke down. George had been asked to help draw up Belgium's rail network, while his son Robert, along with another engineer, Henry Swinburne, was given the same task in Switzerland. Robert also designed the first railway in Africa, a 120-mile (193-km) route connecting the Egyptian port of Alexandria on the Mediterranean with Cairo, which opened in 1856. In Asia, it was support from the British government and money from British investors – who were offered a very generous guaranteed 5 per cent rate of return – that enabled the first railway, a short line that ran from Bombay to a small neighbouring town, Thana, to open in 1853. Russia and Italy* both built their inaugural lines to connect their capital cities with a royal palace (in Russia's case from St Petersburg to the tsar's residence at Tsarskoe Selo). While in Germany,† the first railway line aimed to serve commuters travelling between the towns of Nuremberg and Fürth to relieve pressure on what had become the busiest road in the country.

These lines were invariably quickly followed by others, often on a far bigger scale and increasingly serving passengers – who proved to be a lucrative market – as well as freight. Within a couple of decades several nations could boast thousands of miles of track. In the US, the expansion towards what quickly became the world's biggest railway system was rapid but haphazard. The country embarked on a railway boom that saw a staggering rate of growth: a couple of thousand miles of track in 1840 had grown to more than 30,000, confined to the east, by the outbreak of the Civil War in 1861.

Unlike some European countries, in the US there was no notion of creating a national network. There, as in Britain, lines

---

\* Or, more accurately, the Kingdom of the Two Sicilies, as the state governing the southern part of the Italian peninsula was then known.

† Again, more accurately, the Kingdom of Bavaria.

OVERLEAF  Tver Station of the Moscow–Saint Petersburg Railway (also known as the Nicholas Railway), photographed around 1860. Russia developed its rail network rather late compared with its western European neighbours.

were built on the basis of promoters spotting an opportunity to make money and obtaining permission for construction from the legislature – in America, the regional authority, the state, rather than the federal government. They tended to be short, built by small local companies which had seen a need for a link between a local mine and a river, or between a local market town and perhaps a settlement from which people needed frequent access to its larger neighbour. As reflected in their names, these railroads were a hotchpotch of disconnected lines, such as the tiny Mine Hill & Schuylkill Haven in Pennsylvania, just 2.5 miles (4 km) long, the slightly longer Palmyra & Jacksonburgh in Michigan, and the romantic-sounding Tuscarora & Cold Run Tunnel & Railroad Company, also in Pennsylvania.

The success and profitability of these early lines, which were by and large freight carriers, stimulated interest, but there was some tacit support from the federal government which abolished

import duties on iron used by the railway companies for track construction. Both local and federal governments helped the nascent industry in other ways, too, by providing army personnel to carry out surveys, a very expensive task for promoters. Later the states allocated – or on occasion, gifted – land to the railway companies, and sometimes provided subsidies or other incentives. The rapid rate of construction was helped, too, by the inexpensive way American railroads were built and by the low cost of land.

It was, however, private entrepreneurs who were the driving force behind the extraordinary expansion in the US, and it was their ability to attract local support that ensured their success. The railroads attracted almost universal enthusiasm as people recognized that the arrival of the 'iron road' was likely to stimulate local economic growth. The new technology was also very much in tune with the *zeitgeist*, a 'can do' culture that was at the heart of the nineteenth-century American frontier spirit. The railways expanded agricultural markets, opened up the possibility of employment in nearby towns and encouraged the arrival of immigrants.

These benefits were cannily sold to local people by the railway promoters, who needed not only local support but often funds to invest in their projects. Typically, according to the entertaining railroad historian Stewart H. Holbrook, promoters would win people over to their cause through extremely thorough lobbying campaigns. He cites the case of a mythical but typical town called Brownsville and suggests that the company's first step was to win over an enthusiastic local notable to its cause and then together they would develop the notion that 'what Brownsville needed if it were to share in America's great destiny, was a steam railroad'.[1] A local meeting would be held, carefully stage-managed by the promoters, and then the hard sell would begin. Shares in the nascent company would be offered to the townsfolk with the

The *Adler* (Eagle) locomotive driven by the British driver William Wilson at the opening of the Nuremberg–Fürth Railway in December 1835, the first line built in Germany.

promise of a good rate of return, more meetings would be held and even the Almighty would be invoked as a supporter.

And the railways would not only promise to bring prosperity. According to the promoters, railways would liberate city dwellers from terrible housing conditions and allow them to live further out of town; the same notion would later stimulate the creation of the Metropolitan Railway in London, the world's first underground railway. The railway was seen as an answer to a wide variety of society's ills: education would be improved through the spread of knowledge, and by giving access to seaside towns or mountain villages with lots of fresh air, they would enable improvements in people's health. Moreover, they were seen as democratic in providing cheap travel to all, and so offered equality of opportunity, already a key facet of the American credo.

For the most part, this hard sell was successful, but much of it was in fact unnecessary since the prevailing atmosphere was supportive anyway. The railway was an invention whose time had come and America, with its huge land mass and its entrepreneurial spirit, was fertile territory. As James Ward, another historian of the early railway boom, puts it, 'Promoters used the steam engine as a metaphor for what they thought Americans were and what they were becoming. They frequently discussed parallels between the locomotive and the national character, pointing out that both possess youth, power, speed, single-mindedness and bright prospects.'[2]

In Britain there were a few naysayers, Cassandras who thought the railways were an instrument of the devil. The Romantic poets saw them as an unwanted incursion into their bucolic idyll. William Wordsworth, the poet laureate, waged an unsuccessful battle against the proposed Kendal & Windermere Railway, whose route penetrated his beloved Lake District. He composed a sonnet which he sent to William Gladstone, then President of the Board of Trade, in October 1844, suggesting the whole local

Railways were fêted in music and the arts, as shown by this cover image for the sheet music of the song 'The Rail Road. A Characteristic Divertimento for the Piano Forte', published in 1828.

# THE

# RAIL ROAD,

A Characteristic Divertimento for the

## Piano Forte;

in which is introduced, a variety of

## National and Popular Airs,

composed by

## C. MEINEKE.

## Baltimore,

Published by John Cole.

Price 75 Cents

population was in 'consternation' about the planned railway and lamenting the arrival of the iron road to these unspoilt parts:

> *Is there no nook of English ground secure from rash assault?*
> *And is no nook of English ground secure*
> *From rash assault? Schemes of retirement sown*
> *In youth, and 'mid the busy world kept pure*
> *As when their earliest flowers of hope were blown,*
> *Must perish;—how can they this blight endure?*

Wordsworth would lose his campaign, however. The railway arrived in Kendal in 1846 and reached Windermere a year later.

Aside from these rare opponents, there was an almost universal welcome for the iron road on both sides of the Atlantic. Its arrival in the small towns and villages was often marked by a day's free travel for the local worthies on a special train, and a banquet accompanied by a brass band to which, if they were lucky, all the town's inhabitants would be invited. Schoolchildren would be given the day off and local entrepreneurs made immediate attempts to capitalize on the great event. Potters and glass-blowers would hastily design commemorative memorabilia, but, to save money, used a standardized pattern showing an early engine hauling a single car alongside the ubiquitous motto 'God Speed Thee'. These ornaments assumed pride of place on countless dressers and on innumerable mantelpieces. The local papers gave the event extensive coverage, sometimes creating special supplements. Some warned of the dangers of the new-fangled machine, not least because in many small towns and villages the tracks ran right down Main Street, presenting a far greater hazard than the horses and carts that had previously predominated. But, as the US railway historian George H. Douglas records, most dissenting voices were quickly drowned out: 'Generally ... when the iron horse made its first appearance, the reception was one of breathless expectation and delight. The backers and planners of all the early railroads saw to it that their first demonstration runs were occasions of festivity.'[3]

The railway was also welcomed as an employment opportunity for those in the region who by and large built the early lines. Generally the route would be divided into small sections, perhaps of a mile or so, and contracted out to small local companies, who made use of idle farm labour. In the American South, though, the railways have a darker history, since many of the lines were built using slaves who, according to the author of a seminal book on the role of African-Americans and the railroads, '... constructed most of the antebellum [pre-Civil War, before 1861] South's 8,784-mile [14,136-km] network'.[4] Slaves who worked on the railroads were subjected to even harsher treatment than their counterparts in the cotton fields: they were exposed to greater health risks, experienced more brutality from overseers and, despite the arduous nature of the work, given fewer rations. Slaves were either bought by the railway companies or leased from their owners. Even after the abolition of slavery following the Civil War, the use of convicted felons, who were often the victims of systematic judicial malpractice, to build railroads continued (and went on right up to the end of the century).

Apart from the Baltimore & Ohio, the longer lines, most of which stretched westward from the eastern seaboard, only began to be built in the 1840s. This was not because of a lack of ambition but rather because the use of different gauges by the early railroads made it impossible to create junctions between them. As mentioned in the previous chapter, this lack of gauge standardization was partly born of the railway companies' desire to carve out areas for themselves that their rivals could not enter. However, it was a self-defeating strategy. By the outbreak of the Civil War in 1861, there were no fewer than eleven different gauges – some of them just an inch different – in the North, of which the most common was 4 foot 8½ inches (or 'standard' gauge), and almost as many in the South. A journey between Philadelphia in Pennsylvania and Charleston in Virginia, a trip of 500 miles (800 km), would have involved no fewer than eight changes of gauge.

There is, however, a very interesting philosophical as well as a technical reason for the limited geographical scope of the early American lines. The early settlers focused on the idea of a homestead that was almost entirely self-sufficient. This was in tune with the vision of one of the nation's founding fathers, Thomas Jefferson, whose idyll was a land of small urban factories and self-sufficient rural farms in which clothing was sewn and food conserved by the womenfolk, while the men tilled the fields and hunted wildlife for the pot with guns produced by a local blacksmith. They needed a railway to reach the local market town but were unlikely ever to travel further.

The contrasting vision was that of another founding father, Alexander Hamilton, who envisaged the development of far bigger factories, benefitting from economies of scale and serving much larger areas, which therefore required a greater dependence on efficient transport. This more federalist idea was bound to triumph as it fitted the capitalist ethos that was driving the US towards its establishment as the world's biggest economy. Those who mistakenly thought that supporting a local railway line would improve their prosperity without changing their way of life only realized their error too late. As is the case with twenty-first-century globalization, created by cheap long-distance sea journeys and universal air connections, nothing could stop the spread of the railway. The local line turned into a regional one and then became part of a national network. This process took decades but was inevitable as the forces of capitalism inevitably rode roughshod over those seeking to live out their lives in small settlements oblivious to their wider surroundings.

...

In Britain, the other country where railways were built through a system of private funding with no government guidance on the design of the network, there was an even sharper period of excess, commonly known as the 'railway mania'. By 1840, in a remarkable first decade of railway construction, around 2,000 miles (3,200 km) of track had been laid, equating to 200 completed miles (320 km) every year since the opening of the Liverpool & Manchester. Nearly all those lines were steam-hauled, and increasingly their principal purpose was the carriage of passengers. However, growth had stalled at the end of the decade. After a mini-boom in the late 1830s, when numerous bills for new lines were presented to Parliament as aspiring promoters took note of the handsome returns of some of the pioneers, there was a lull until the spring of 1844 followed by a second explosion of interest. This came about partly because of a general improvement in the economic situation. Railway company shares were again doing particularly well and numerous promoters were eager to cash in on the boom, by enticing the burgeoning middle class to put their savings into schemes that promised a high rate of return. Alongside many perfectly honest entrepreneurs, however, there were numerous crooks, whose sole purpose was to relieve investors of their money.

All the new railway schemes had to be presented to Parliament for scrutiny, but this was often cursory as suddenly the trickle of bills became a flood and the legislators were overwhelmed. The bare figures are remarkable. After the first boom collapsed, the lean years from 1838 to 1843 saw just 50 miles (80 km) of new railway lines authorized, but then in 1844 alone Parliamentary approval was given to 800 miles (1,300 km) of track. The fact that these new railways entailed the passing of as many as forty-eight acts shows that most of the new lines were very short. But this was only the start. Over the next two years things really did go crazy, as Parliament approved a further 6,200 miles (10,000 km) of railway – more than a trebling of the existing network. In total, just under 10,000 miles (16,000 km) were approved from 1844 to 1847, equivalent to nearly the whole of Britain's rail network today. Only two-thirds of these lines were actually built, and inevitably many people lost a lot of money on schemes that failed or turned out to be fraudulent. The eventual bursting of the bubble of railway mania was not down to any particular incident but simply because the assessments of the money to be made proved to be wildly over-optimistic. By that time virtually everyone with a few pounds to invest had acquired railway shares, including – according to *Punch* magazine – Queen Victoria herself. The vast majority of these individuals lost out, triggering a sharp downturn in the British economy.

While many critics have argued, in retrospect, that the railway boom of the 1840s was a haphazard and wasteful process, it undoubtedly resulted in the building of a large number of railway lines, most of which survive to this day. Parliament did make a half-hearted attempt to control the process with an act, passed in 1844, which allowed for the appointment of a board of five commissioners. Under the chairmanship of Lord Dalhousie, who as India's Governor-General would go on to establish the first railways in Asia, the board was supposed to scrutinize the flood of bills and reject schemes designed to block other more legitimate railways or which offered few benefits to the public. However, one element of the commission's brief, namely to discourage unnecessary competition, would lead to a conflict in economic policy, since there was a widespread dislike of the larger railway companies and their attempts to impose monopolies over the regions they covered. The Victorians were torn over whether competition or co-ordination should be the guiding economic principle, an issue that was never effectively resolved. Therefore, while some mergers were later approved, others were rejected precisely because of the fear of railway monopolies. The commission did manage to rationalize a few bills on a regional basis but overall its powers, which were only advisory – the government being reluctant to constrain private enterprise – were too limited for it to make much real difference. Its paltry efforts seemed increasingly to be out of sync with the *zeitgeist* and within a few years the commission was disbanded. *Laissez-faire* was now the rule of the day. An analysis of the railway mania published in the 1930s sums up the failings of the commission well:

> The very qualified acceptance of the advice tendered by Dalhousie's board in the proceedings during the session of 1845, and the absence of any co-ordinating force during those of 1846 had resulted in the railway map of the country being traced with a network of lines whose only common object was the prospect of material gain to the prospective shareholders of the individual companies concerned.[5]

London, though, proved to be an exception to the *laissez-faire* approach and this has had a lasting impact on the development of the UK's capital city. Dalhousie enters our story again, this time as chairman of the Royal Commission on Metropolis Railway Termini which was set up in 1845 to consider the various proposals for lines and stations in London. In the kind of state planning process that was largely anathema to the Victorians, the commission rejected plans for a central station serving all points of the compass, which had been proposed for Farringdon, on the grounds that it would have required too much demolition of property.* Instead, the commission created a kind of no-go

---

* One cannot resist imagining what an amazing facility it would have been. Oddly enough, the Victorians' vision for Farringdon will be partly realized when Crossrail, London's new east–west commuter railway, eventually opens. Together with Thameslink, Crossrail will give passengers at Farringdon direct access to services across the whole of southern Britain.

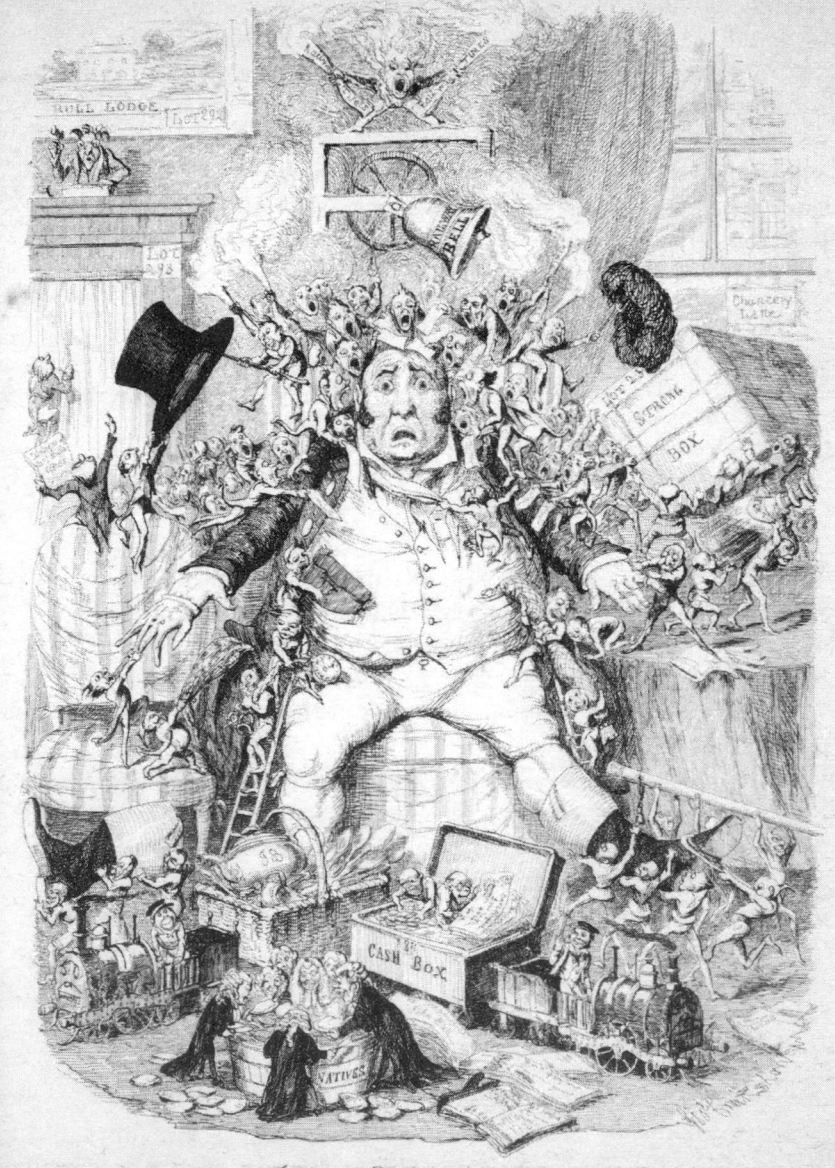

Mr. John Bull in a Quandary.
or
The anticipated effects of the Railway calls.

area encompassing much of the City and the West End where railways were not allowed. This directive resulted in London's mainline stations being built on a ring around this area, linked by the Underground's Circle Line,* whose construction was recommended by the commission. It is notable that when Dalhousie went to India and pushed the British government to support the establishment of railways there, he insisted that there should be an overall plan for them. He personally drew up a map that became the core of the Indian rail network, though it would take half a century for it to come to fruition.

While in Britain and America the rush to build railways was stimulated by the private sector, in other countries it was governments that led the surge. In France, for example, there was encouragement by the state to build narrow-gauge lines into almost every village. In Germany and Italy, not yet unified countries at the time when the iron horse was first emerging, the railways were deployed as a unifying force, a way of creating a sense of nationhood. By the middle of the nineteenth century, every advanced nation was either building or planning to build a railway network. It was a time of rapid change, and the effects were almost unlimited.

---

* The circle of Underground lines linking London's mainline termini was not completed until 1884, but did not actually acquire its modern name of the 'Circle Line' until 1949.

The railways attracted much criticism and were often the subject of satirical illustrations such as this one, showing John Bull overwhelmed by the effects of this novel invention.

# Changing the World

The Great Exhibition of 1851, held in London's Hyde Park, marked the beginning of the globalization that was the inevitable outcome of the Industrial Revolution. Its full name, 'The Great Exhibition of the Works of Industry of All Nations', demonstrates the ambition of its organizer, Prince Albert, the Prince Consort, and it became the first of a series of world fairs which showed off the latest developments in industry and culture from all the most economically advanced nations.

It is no coincidence that the exhibition was held just as the rail network had become extensive enough to enable much of the population to travel to London quickly and relatively cheaply. The exhibition was, by a huge margin, the greatest mass event held in Great Britain up to that time. Indeed, in terms of the proportion of the population that it attracted, the success of the Great Exhibition has arguably never been surpassed.

Over a period of some six months, between 1 May and 15 October 1851, the exhibition was attended by 6.2 million visitors, representing one-third of Britain's total population at the time. Two-thirds of these benefitted from the cheap, one shilling* fares on offer, and without the railway network, few would have been able to make the journey. While the cheapest way to reach the exhibition was by special excursion trains – often organized by town or even village 'Exhibition Clubs' – reduced-price tickets were also made available on many scheduled services. The railway companies were slow to grasp the business opportunity afforded by the Great Exhibition. At first, they had tried to stick to previously agreed rules designed to stop companies reducing fares to compete against each other, which they realized would wreck any hopes of profit. However, as soon as the railways became alive to the exhibition's potential, the companies began to offer special fares. For example, a return from Sheffield or Leeds to London cost just five shillings*. Cheap travel was also available

---

\* The equivalent of about £5 in today's money.

in the form of the so-called 'Parliamentary trains' specified by the 1844 Railway Regulation Act, which required every railway company to run at least one train per day on every route at a fare of just one penny a mile. However, angered by this imposition through legislation, some companies deliberately scheduled these services at inconvenient times of the day so that few people could take advantage of them.

While excursion trains and 'specials' to sporting events opened up a host of opportunities for travel and leisure, the railways also left a profound and permanent imprint on both town and country. Country-dwellers, perhaps, felt the strongest initial impact as their way of life was changed forever. Consider a rural area suddenly connected with the local town and thence to the rest of the country. The effect was immediate. Local people now had access to much wider markets to fulfil their needs. They no longer had to travel by road to purchase chickens, piglets and calves to replenish their livestock. Feed for these animals became cheaper as transport costs were reduced. And when they were fattened up, they could be taken to market by train, ensuring they kept more of their weight. Supplies of fertilizer and seed could also be brought in more easily. Crucially, the price of coal fell on average by one-third, allowing homes to be heated more cheaply. Further afield, the department stores in London and other big cities recognized that they now had the means of accessing places that had hitherto been beyond their reach and their mail-order businesses expanded rapidly as a result. But it was not all upside. Easier access to the local market town might well spell doom for small village shops. The higher prices that agricultural produce obtained on a wider market could push prices up for local people or even cause shortages. When the railways of Devon and Cornwall expanded in the 1860s, reaching many previously isolated villages and hamlets, so much milk was exported to other parts of the country that it became scarce in the West Country and disrupted the local dairy business. Nevertheless, the overall impact of the railways on rural life was in many ways a positive óne. Agriculture became more efficient thanks to the greater availability of fertilizer and machinery, and farmers' ability to sell their produce to customers far outside their immediate region contributed to increased revenue.

The cheaper production of food greatly benefitted urban dwellers, and produce could arrive at markets fresher and from further afield. Once refrigeration on trains was introduced, the milk that was collected from West Country farmers could be sold in distant places such as London which previously had been reliant on farms nearby or, worse, cows living in basements. Apart from clearing out the cows, the railways fundamentally changed the nature of urban life in many other ways too. While there had been suburbs before the railways, these had generally been inhabited by people retiring from the hubbub of the city to seek a quieter life. The coming of the railways stimulated a vast expansion of these areas, which became dormitory towns for workers who travelled daily into town. Here the railways were partly responsible for entrenching class distinctions. London's first railway, the London & Greenwich – which opened in 1836 – was specifically designed, according to its shareholder prospectus, to ensure that the new inhabitants living near the new stations 'can be conveyed [at speed] from the smoke of the city to the pure air of Blackheath and Shooter's Hill'.[1] And, the prospectus continued, the railway would enable 'thousands of labourers [to] sleep in cheap lodgings at a distance from town, and yet carry on their daily labour at a loss of only 6d [sixpence] per day', which was the proposed return fare.

The London & Greenwich soon became a successful railway, and others followed swiftly in its wake, serving places in south London such as Surbiton, Bromley and Croydon. But it was in the second half of the century that railway construction in the capital would lead to an explosion in growth of its outer suburbs. Suburbs serving different classes were developed according to the type of trains available. Some companies, such as the Great Northern operating out of King's Cross and the Great Western, which ran trains out of Paddington, paid little heed to their suburban hinterlands, so that only the affluent, who could afford high fares and were relaxed about the low frequency of trains, were content to rely on their services to live in places such as Hornsey and Ealing. By contrast, the Great Eastern, operating from Liverpool Street, provided a plethora of trains, and much cheap housing was built around its stations to provide accommodation for low-paid workers in areas such as Walthamstow, Leyton and Enfield. These workmen's trains were introduced very early on in the development of Britain's railways. They offered a reduced rate for travel at particular times, sometimes with the fares graded so that very early services, aimed at manual workers, were cheaper than the slightly later ones used by clerks and other white-collar workers. The first service offering cheap workmen's fares was provided by the Eastern Counties Railway for dockers in the Port of London in 1847 and it was followed five years later by the Stockton & Darlington, by then a modern railway operated by locomotives, which ran services for workers to the iron-working village of Eston in north Yorkshire.

The Metropolitan Railway, the first London Underground line, opened in 1863 and, realizing that there was massive potential for carrying people to and from their workplace, its owners offered day returns at just threepence rather than ninepence. Henry Mayhew, a social researcher and early supporter of the Metropolitan Railway, travelled on the line on a workmen's train and was impressed with both the quality of the carriages and the large number and variety of people they were carrying. Despite the early hour, there was 'a bustle with men, a large number of who had bass baskets in their hands or tin flagons or basins done

OVERLEAF The 4-mile-long London & Greenwich Railway was the world's first suburban railway. It was built on 851 arches which still carry a major railway today. The first section was opened in 1836.

up in red handkerchiefs. Some who carried large saws under their arms were carpenters… whilst some were habited in the grey and clay stained fustian suit peculiar to ground labourers.'[2] This was long before the days of hi-vis vests and hard hats. The Metropolitan's rival, the Metropolitan District Railway (originally established in 1864) expanded to the west and south covering villages and small towns such as Putney, Wimbledon, Acton and Chiswick with frequent services and cheap fares that led to rapid population increases in all the areas it covered.

It was not only housing developments that were stimulated by the railway. Industry in riverside suburbs such as Brentford and Tilbury expanded greatly thanks to their being served by the railway. London owed much of its rapid expansion to its burgeoning railway network.

Other towns and cities in Britain also developed transport networks, mostly a combination of trams and trains, to serve their burgeoning suburbs and industrial areas. Some of these, for instance in Leeds, Birmingham and Liverpool, have survived, while others have been lost in post-Second World War cutbacks resulting from the 'Beeching Axe' * of the 1960s.

…

The process of suburbanization was replicated in the United States. But because land outside American cities was often more readily available and cheaper to purchase, the spread of built-up areas was far greater than in Britain. This was natural territory for the railways, which were able to lay out tracks cheaply both to serve the existing suburbs and to stimulate the creation of new ones. The very word 'commuter' was in fact first used in the 1840s when local rail services around major US cities such as New York,

* See page 199 for discussion of the Beeching Report and the ensuing cuts in the railway network.

PREVIOUS PAGES London has more major terminuses than any city in the world. This is one of the earliest, Paddington, designed by Isambard Kingdom Brunel (1806–59), showing people waiting for a train to take them to the Henley rowing regatta in July 1908.

Philadelphia, Boston and Chicago were being created with the idea of serving suburban dwellers working there. Some of the railroads offered these regular passengers 'commuted' tickets. The initial take-up was poor except in Boston, where some eighty-five commuter stations were soon built within 15 miles (24 km) of the city centre.

It was not until the 1880s, with the rapid growth of many railroads in the suburbs, that the habit of commuting by rail became widely established. As George H. Douglas, a chronicler of this phenomenon, put it, 'Suburban railroad traffic changed the American landscape in the 1880s and 1890s [forging] a new kind of link between the city's core and the pastoral environs that had once been thought [of] as far away.'[3] The railroads both created the early suburbs, stimulating growth wherever there was a station, and determined the rhythm of life, which became ruled by the clock and, specifically, the railway timetable. Office hours were determined by the arrival of trains, creating the nine-to-five working day and establishing routines that were adhered to daily for years: commuters often sitting in the same carriages, perhaps even the same seat, on the same train with the same paper and, quite likely, the same conductor checking the tickets. The railroads, in other words, created the prison of timekeeping. The railway companies also tried to keep changes to a minimum. The Lackawanna Railroad, which ran services in the region around New York, can lay claim to have operated the longest-running US commuter train service, the 16.15 from its Hoboken terminal in New Jersey non-stop to the leafy towns of Madison and Morristown. The train started operating in 1883 and lasted until 1970, when it was discontinued as the company restructured, much to the consternation of its most faithful user, the copper-mining executive and one-time mayor of Morristown, W. Parsons Todd, who had commuted on the train to his office in New York since 1899.

OVERLEAF The Metropolitan District Railway between Paddington to Blackfriars via Kensington was built between 1866 and 1870 after the immediate success of the world's first underground, the Metropolitan Railway, using the same cut and cover technique which caused much disruption.

...

It was not only the nine-to-fivers who needed to know the precise railway timetable. The requirement for railways to stick to a clear timetable, to ensure that passengers reached their destinations at the expected hour, resulted in time, which had been a local concept, being standardized within and across countries. In Britain, before the arrival of the railways, towns had kept their own time according to their latitude. The time in Plymouth, for example, was twenty minutes later than in London, but since transport was so slow this hardly mattered to the stagecoach passenger who had spent nearly a day getting there from the capital. But the advent of a complex network of railways used by many passengers who required connections created the necessity for precision and punctuality. Once the main east–west railway, the Great Western, began to expand westwards, confusion over train timings led the company to push for standardization based on Greenwich Mean Time. Its efforts to persuade Parliament to adopt a UK-wide time initially failed, however, and therefore, in 1841, the company unilaterally introduced its own standardized timetable based on Greenwich Mean Time but retaining some local variations. Thus Reading was four minutes behind London, Chippenham eight minutes and Bristol fourteen. This was, in fact, still pretty confusing and so a decade later, the company standardized time throughout its network. Other railways, pressed by the industry's co-ordinating body, the Railway Clearing House (established in 1842), quickly followed suit, but it was not until 1880 that Parliament decided that the rest of the country should standardize clocks. Until then in most places in the UK the local church clocks would show a different time from those at the station, which stimulated the railway companies to erect giant clocks on their station façades. Norwich and Shrewsbury had particularly magnificent clocks – symbolic statements of the railway companies' power. They saw themselves as above the law of the local authorities – whose town halls were often far less imposing than the local railway station – and even of God, for people had previously relied on the church clock.

America, too, had eventually to yield to the chronological discipline of the railway, though there was more resistance on that side of the Atlantic and consequently standardized time took rather longer to establish. While modernizers were keen to introduce a series of time zones, which of course were necessary given America's vast size, a group known as the 'obscurantists' were strongly resistant as they thought that the sun ought to determine the time throughout the country. It took until 1869 for the movement for a zonal system to begin to take root. The leading lobbyist for change was William Frederick Allen, the former engineer of one of the early major railroads, the Camden & Amboy, whose efforts are immortalized on a tablet in Washington, DC's delightful Union station. He suggested four time zones and this was adopted at a convention in 1883, but there was still resistance. In Bangor, Maine, in the northeastern corner of the country, Mayor Dogberry refused to accept a city ordinance to adopt Eastern Standard Time, arguing it was 'unconstitutional, being an attempt to change the immutable laws of God Almighty',[4] and he banned local sextons from ringing the bells at the newly established times. More significantly, while the railway companies did not fear God's wrath but were delighted, the introduction of the new timings on a network that had previously used local times presented no little danger. It was decided that at noon on the appointed day all trains would stop *en route* while the timetables were adjusted. While no accidents occurred, there were innumerable delays and confusion continued for several months. In Russia, the Trans-Siberian Railway uses Moscow time along its whole 5,750-mile (9,250-km) length, which can cause confusion for unaccustomed passengers, but any alternative method would be even more confusing on a railway that cuts across seven time zones.*

...

For most of the nineteenth century, the spread of the railways across the world was so rapid and so influential that it is hard to discern ways in which people's lives were *not* transformed by its arrival. The advent of the railways led to changes in diet, housing, food and numerous other aspects of people's lives and more widely, the economy and even the way that people were governed.

Excursion trains had become an established feature of the railways even before the Great Exhibition. The first recorded example of group travel was an outing by 150 Sunday School teachers on the Liverpool & Manchester Railway soon after it opened in 1830. Before long monster trains were carrying thousands of people on outings and day trips. In August 1840, almost 3,000 people travelled from Nottingham to Leicester for a day out in a train that reportedly had 67 carriages; four years later, 6,600 travelled from Leeds to Hull in 240 carriages hauled by nine locomotives, but it is unknown whether this was in a single train or a series of them. The very concept of the bank holiday trip to the seaside was a product of the railways. In the 1830s, the number of saints' days observed as holidays in Britain was significantly reduced, and a lesser number of public holidays (later to be known as 'bank holidays') established. The railways enabled people to take day trips to the seaside on these days, something that would not have been possible before. Week-long holidays soon became commonplace. For example, in one holiday week in August 1850, more than 200,000 left Manchester by various excursion trains. In the US, too, the railway companies

---

* During the Soviet period, even meals on the trains were served at Moscow time, which meant breakfast could be at lunchtime, but this is no longer the case.

were quick to encourage a form of travel that they recognized as a useful source of income. In the mid-1830s, the Boston & Worcester Railroad in Massachusetts ran 4th of July specials, carrying 1,500 people on four trains.

These enormous movements of people gave the masses a taste of freedom and instilled a widespread desire for travel, which could only be met by the railways. Writing in 1852, F. S. Williams noted: 'Men who but a few years since scarcely crossed the precincts of the country in which they were born, and knew as little of the general features of the land of their birth as they did the topography of the moon, now unhesitatingly avail themselves of the means of communication that are afforded.'[5]

Unscheduled excursion trains were, however, particularly prone to disaster – partly because of the huge numbers on board but also because they ran at unusual times, and occasionally took signallers by surprise. The world's first major rail accident occurred near Paris in May 1842 and involved a train carrying day-trippers who had travelled to Versailles for celebrations in honour of King Louis Philippe. The train's seventeen coaches were packed with 770 passengers. Disaster struck on the return journey in the evening, when the axle on one of the two locomotives broke, causing the train to derail. At least fifty passengers – some estimates suggest as many as 200 – perished in the ensuing conflagration after the engines' coals set fire to the wooden carriages. Many of those who died had survived the initial crash unscathed, but were trapped inside the carriages and unable to escape the blaze. The Versailles derailment led to the end of the practice of routinely locking passengers in their compartments, which until then had been widespread in Europe. In Britain a number of early railway accidents also involved special trains. In 1861 sixteen passengers on a 'special' were killed at Kentish Town when their train collided with a freight service as a result of a mistake by a young signaller.

In one of those symbiotic developments that are difficult to untangle, the seaside towns that were the destination for many of these excursions expanded rapidly as a result of the crowds that now flocked to them by rail. Towns and villages with no railway access, but which boasted a nice stretch of beach or some handsome cliffs, clamoured to be connected to the network. In 1840, Fleetwood in Lancashire became the first seaside town to acquire a railway station, and Weston-super-Mare in Somerset followed the next year. By the end of the decade, more than a dozen others had joined the railway age, giving the excursion trains a far wider choice of destination.

While the northern resorts of Scarborough and Blackpool represented the summit of possible holiday destinations for Britain's working classes, the more affluent could choose to spend their winters on the Côte d'Azur, or French Riviera, as the British called it. Cross-Channel ferries were soon connecting south coast towns such as Dover and Brighton with their French equivalents, making it feasible for the middle classes to take trips abroad. The passengers would often reach their destinations using the services of Thomas Cook, whose company became synonymous with long-distance travel. Cook has been frequently, but wrongly, credited with inventing the concept of the excursion train – in fact they had existed for a decade before he ran his first trip on 5 July 1841 – but he did much to popularize railway holiday travel. That first excursion took 570 people just 11 miles (17.7 km) from Leicester to Loughborough to attend a teetotal rally where lunch, dancing and other activities were provided in the private park of a fellow active supporter of the temperance movement. It was Cook's desire to provide activities to deter people from seeking the solace of the pub that, at least initially, motivated him to develop his rail travel business. The enterprise was soon carrying people abroad and even, in 1872, on a Jules Verne-type trip around the world – though at 212 days (at a cost of £210

A poster advertising the fast trains to the Kent ports of Folkestone and Dover which connected with rapid steamer sailings to France. The company, better known as the London, Chatham & Dover, began running passenger services between Dover and Calais in 1864.

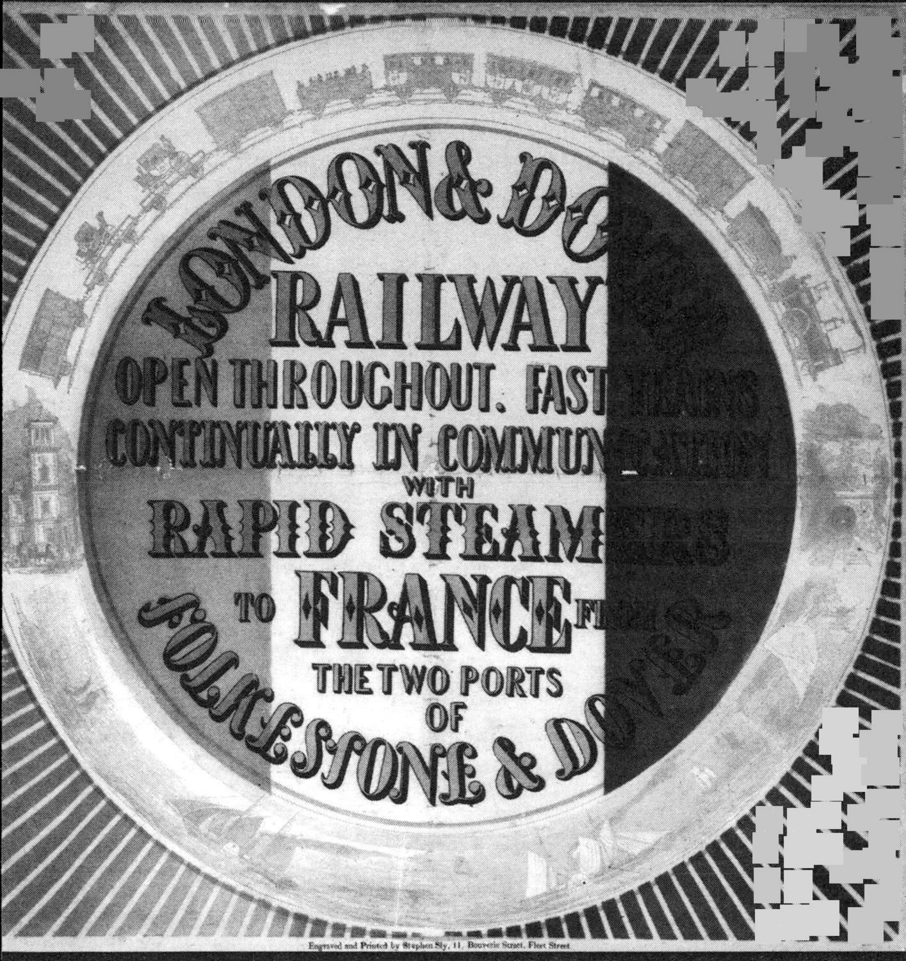

LONDON & DO...

RAILWAY

OPEN THROUGHOUT. FAST TRAINS

CONTINUALLY IN COMMUN...

WITH

RAPID STEAMERS

TO FRANCE FROM

THE TWO PORTS

OF

FOLKESTONE & DOVER

Engraved and Printed by Stephen Sly, 11, Bouverie Street, Fleet Street or £25,000 in today's values) it took rather longer than Phileas Fogg's effort in Jules Verne's *Around the World in Eighty Days*, a book that was published in the following year. Much later, just before the First World War, Henry Flagler, an affluent and philanthropic US oilman, used much of his fortune to develop railways on the coast of Florida in order to service the hotels he built there. His crowning achievement, completed in 1912, was the construction of a 128-mile (206-km) line reaching far out into the Atlantic Ocean, over rocky islands and long stretches of sea, to connect Key West, Ernest Hemingway's favourite haunt, with the mainland.

Better access to the sea changed people's diets, too, as the railways were responsible for the spread of what soon became Britain's favourite dish, fish and chips. Fried fish had long been a staple in seaside towns, but before the advent of the railways fresh fish was not available in inland areas because of the slowness of the transport system. Having discovered the joys of cheap fish on their jaunts to seaside resorts, the urban masses were a ready market once trains started to be used to transport fishermen's catches rapidly to towns and cities across the country. The trains were thus significant in two ways, both through giving people the opportunity to taste fish but also by enabling its cheap transport. For example, almost as soon as the railway line to Yarmouth, on the Norfolk coast, was opened in 1844, it began to transport fish inland to Norwich and further afield. The first fish and chip shops were established in the 1860s. By the start of the First World War there were 25,000 of these takeaway shops across the country, served by the local fish markets that had become established in major towns and cities.

It was not only sea air, fish and chips and jolly holidays that attracted people onto the railways. In Cornwall, in Britain's southwest, the Bodmin & Wadebridge Railway ran a very crowded excursion train to a public double hanging at Bodmin in

August 1840. Nine years later a whole fleet of trains, with special fares being offered by the rail companies, brought in many of the 100,000-strong crowd who watched the hanging of the multiple murderer John Gleeson Wilson outside Kirkdale jail in Liverpool in September 1849.*

The illegal sport of prize-fighting, which involved men pummelling each other with their bare fists, was another mid-century attraction in the UK, which the railways for a time actively encouraged because of the business it brought them. Whereas prize-fighting had long predated the advent of the railways, the ability to travel to matches by train provided opportunities for fights to take place in remote places from which special trains could spirit away the combatants and the crowds. Mobs of spectators sometimes piled onto trains with magistrates in hot pursuit. This might result in a fight being stopped in one place, only to be resumed further down the tracks over a county boundary beyond the jurisdiction of the chasing officials. Simon Bradley, in his masterly account of the impact of the railways in Great Britain, raises an eyebrow at how the railways connived in this unlawful activity: 'Although it was not illegal to attend such events, the readiness with which the railway companies joined in the traffic is startling – as if British Rail had laid on special trains to the ecstasy-fuelled farmland raves of the 1980s.'[6]

The railways proved a boon for more legitimate activities such as horseracing. Again the relationship was a symbiotic one, which brought about changes to both railways and racing. Soon after the opening of the Liverpool & Manchester Railway, racegoers

---

* The sightseers were 'treated' to the awful sight of a bungled execution which took fifteen minutes as the poor wretch strangled to death because the drop had been too short. Even worse, the headcap fell off, revealing Wilson's bulging eyes and his purple face. Executions were no longer a source of revenue for the railways after 1868 as they were then carried out in the privacy of the prison grounds.

were using the line to reach the course at Newton-le-Willows, the predecessor to Haydock Park. The London & Southampton Railway was quick to follow suit, laying on special trains for racegoers bound for Epsom. However, it underestimated demand. On the first race day after the line opened in 1838, more than 5,000 disappointed racing enthusiasts were left milling around its terminus at Nine Elms in south London, unable to board any of the eight special trains bound for the racecourse. This rail-borne influx of *hoi polloi* was not always welcome to the elitist members of the Jockey Club who preferred traditional small meetings at country courses accessible only to those who could ride their own horses there. However, the numbers who flooded to race meetings by rail changed the whole nature of racing, turning it into a mass sport – whether the Jockey Club liked it or not. As Bradley recounts, 'Before the South Yorkshire Railway opened in 1849, Sheffield people without access to a horse or carriage could only travel the 18 miles [29 km] to the Doncaster course on foot – which meant walking all through the night.'[7] In contrast, in 1910, the four-day meeting was serviced by no fewer than 1,065 special services from all four corners of the country, which necessitated setting up special temporary signal boxes to cope with the extra traffic.

The railways also facilitated the expansion – and consequently the growth in popularity – of other sports. The arrival of the first Australian touring cricket team in 1878 attracted huge crowds, many of whom travelled on railway specials. The establishment a decade later of the English Football League, which encompassed a dozen teams from the north and the midlands, was made possible by the railways, which enabled the clubs, and their supporters, to travel easily to away games. The county cricket championship, which included teams as far apart as Yorkshire and Sussex, was inaugurated in 1890 and also attracted huge crowds travelling by rail.

The way the railways affected baseball in the US was more subtle. The game originally became popular during the Civil War and when the first professional league was created in the 1870s, Chicago and Boston were the leading teams. Clearly the only way teams and supporters could travel between their respective cities was by train. Indeed, the geographic scope of the league was actually dictated by the railways. For several decades, the westernmost big league team was the St Louis Cardinals whose city was the furthest point west that could be reached in an overnight journey from the east coast. These long railway journeys were an established feature of life for the baseball players and a whole culture of life on the train, involving many practical jokes, evolved over the years. It was only when travel by air became commonplace in the 1950s that the league could expand beyond the midwest, allowing the Dodgers franchise, for example, to be relocated from Brooklyn to Los Angeles.

The railways helped other US sports to expand too. When the professional leagues of basketball and American football developed after the First World War, the railways enabled them to extend their geographical reach. College football teams had long used the railway to travel to key matches against local rivals and New England's main railroad company, the New Haven, provided special trains every year between New Haven and Boston for the matches between Yale and Harvard. Right up to the 1950s, golf tournaments also attracted large crowds – as well as the star players of the day such as Ben Hogan and Bobby Jones – onto the rails.

Perhaps less predictably, the creation of the railways resulted in a huge expansion of cultural events. In Britain, theatre companies, some set up for just a single tour, were able to go round the country to perform for a week each at a series of venues. The cast and all the support staff would move from one town to another on a Sunday, taking with them all the props and costumes. The

OVERLEAF The railways were great facilitators of sport as they enabled away teams like the touring Indian Cricket Team of 1932, shown here at Victoria Station, to travel long distances for matches.

railway companies had initially, under pressure from religious organizations, been reluctant to run trains on the sabbath, especially in the mornings when their services might conflict with more Godly ones, but gradually they relented, offering a restricted but adequate timetable, and they later provided special trains for theatre company moves. This was big business. By the end of the nineteenth century, there were on average 142 Sunday theatre special trains each week in England and Wales, carrying hundreds of performers and support staff to new digs in time for Monday night's show. For London theatres, too, the railways provided a massive boost. Commuters, particularly from the growing – and well rail-connected – south London suburbs could use their season tickets at weekends to travel up to town to see a play, and then catch the last train home. With considerably expanded audiences, the theatres could have longer runs and use more expensive sets. Other British cities with suburban networks, such as Manchester and Glasgow, also became cultural centres thanks to improved transport opportunities that allowed people to travel to the theatre and return home late at night by rail.

This new-found mobility also impacted on British musical life. In Wales, the railways transformed the National Eisteddfod into a mass event and subsequently helped spread and consolidate the Welsh tradition of choral singing. The Crystal Palace built for the Great Exhibition was moved to south London and became the largest venue for concerts in Britain. In June 1859, five years after its reopening, an audience of 81,000 people heard a choir of 2,700 sing Handel's *Messiah* at a concert to mark the centenary of the composer's death. To cater for these enormous crowds, two stations were developed to serve the palace, and the intimate relationship between the railways and such events is demonstrated by the fact that every printed concert programme included a timetable of trains suitable for the return journey.

In the arena of entertainment, perhaps the railway's most

difficult task was the carriage of whole circuses. The railway made nationwide tours of circuses feasible, but carrying them was a complicated matter, requiring special carriages for trainers to coax animals such as lions and elephants onto trains without undue anxiety. Circus trains were originally an American idea; in the 1850s several circuses adopted the railways as the best means of moving from venue to venue. Soon, to facilitate journeys across longer distances, special wagons with adjustable axles to cope with the diverse gauges used across America were deployed. In the 1870s Barnum & Bailey became the first circus to put its entire show, animals and all, on a train and advertise themselves as 'railroad shows'. In 1873, W. W. Cole's Famous New York & New Orleans Circus became the first to make use of the Transcontinental line, which had opened in 1869, and toured the West Coast with a thirty-five-car train that travelled just under 10,000 miles (16,093 km).

Workers building the First Transcontinental Railroad gathered around the locomotive *Jupiter*, c.1869.

These circus trains were impressive sights in their own right, and were very much part of the publicity campaign for the show itself. They often consisted of two whole trains, which were unloaded and reloaded with military precision: 'Chutes were placed in the doors of the stock cars for the unloading of the baggage horses (work horses), elephants, zebras and camels. Within the hour, the first section of the circus train had been unloaded and work was progressing on the second.'[8] Large numbers of people would come to the stations to watch this intricate process unfold.

Moving circuses was always a difficult enterprise, and the circus trains experienced several bad accidents. In the presence of so much combustible material, fires were inevitable and frequent. Most of them caused damage only to property, but several led to fatalities. The highest death toll occurred at Hammond, Indiana,

in June 1918, when the Hagenbeck-Wallace circus train was hit by an empty troop train whose engineer had fallen asleep. The ensuing fire, triggered by the circus train's oil lamps igniting the wooden cars, killed 86 people as well as numerous circus animals, and injured 127 others.

The American circus train even reached Britain. When Barnum & Bailey toured Europe from 1898 to 1902, the circus used four trains, each with seventeen wagons, specially built in Stoke-on-Trent. Later the same vehicles were used for Buffalo Bill's Wild West tour, which went round Britain for three years.

Right up to the 1960s in the UK and until 2017 in the US, trains carried circuses – like the Ringling Brothers Circus shown here – from venue to venue.

British circuses, by contrast, tended to remain at fixed venues. It was only in the 1930s that the circus owner Bertram Mills decided to use the railways for touring, using a series of trains comprising as many as seventy-five wagons. This was, however, not a success for either the railways or the circus, and the trains were abandoned before the outbreak of the Second World War. Ringling Bros and Barnum & Bailey, the successor company to the circus that started using the railway as its principal form of transport in the 1870s, stopped travelling across the US by train only in May 2017.

...

It was not only the living who made use of the railways. The coffins of those who died away from home were routinely loaded onto goods wagons, a phenomenon so commonplace that major stations kept a trolley dedicated to the purpose. Death, though, was also good business. In 1854, the all-too-honestly named London Necropolis Railway started running trains to carry the recently deceased and their mourners to a newly opened cemetery at Brookwood in Surrey, 25 miles (40 km) from the centre of London. Its sister company, the London Necropolis Company, had spotted a potential business opportunity in the shortage of burial grounds after the deadly cholera epidemic of 1848–9. However, the company realized it would need to provide transport to its huge new cemetery, which its publicity claimed was large enough to accommodate all the deaths in London for centuries to come.* In order to offer some privacy for the mourners, a new station was established next to the recently opened Waterloo station, with numerous private rooms to accommodate them as they waited for their train. The business expanded quickly, with separate

---

* My own mother, who died in 1999, is in fact buried in the small Swedish section there.

trains run for different religious denominations as well as for the three different classes of deceased. Trains known by railway workers as 'stiffs expresses' carried up to forty-eight corpses at a time. At Brookwood, there were separate stations for Anglicans and Nonconformists, the latter having to settle for burial on the chillier north side of the cemetery. Although the company was over-optimistic in its prediction and never established the domination it hoped for, the service survived until the Second World War when the Necropolis station, which had been resited in 1902 to the Westminster bridge side of Waterloo station, was severely damaged in a raid by the Luftwaffe.

While the lower and middle classes were despatched to Brookwood, the great and the good had rather more luxurious final journeys. Indeed, the tradition of grand railway send-offs for prime ministers and royalty lasted for more than a century. The Duke of Wellington, who died at Walmer Castle in Kent in September 1852, had in life disliked travelling by rail, but there was no alternative but to transport his dead body from the Kent coast to London by train. The journey to St Paul's Cathedral was undertaken by the local train company, the South Eastern Railway, amid much fanfare. One hundred and thirteen years later, Sir Winston Churchill's last journey, following his funeral service at St Paul's, was to Hanborough in Oxfordshire, a short distance away from his final resting-place at Bladon, near Blenheim. Churchill's train had the added cachet of being hauled by an eponymous locomotive which was, appropriately, a Battle of Britain class engine.

# Nationbuilding

While the lives of individuals were transformed in so many ways by the advent of the railways, their introduction also led to fundamental changes in society, notably in strengthening the concept of the nation-state, making possible the waging of longer and bloodier wars and extending the reach and capacity of capitalism.

Belgium's rulers were the first to realize the potential of the railways in unifying their nation. The country was formed in 1830 when the mainly Catholic southern provinces of the Netherlands succeeded in detaching themselves from their Protestant-dominated Dutch neighbours. Inevitably, its transport network was wholly inadequate as it had not been designed for the needs of an independent nation. The Belgian railway was both planned and owned by the state although built by private enterprise, and, as with so many railways, the military's needs were taken into account in its design.

The separation of Holland and Belgium had left the latter with no access to the main waterways that were the lifeblood of the transport system, so the fledgling nation was at risk of being blockaded in the event of a conflict. As Germany was its main trading partner, an alternative to the waterways that had connected what was now Belgium with the Rhine was needed. In

1834 Leopold I, the first king of Belgium, approved plans to build a rail network and the first line between Brussels and Mechelen was completed the following year. With such strong government support for the construction of the railways, the complaints of troublesome landowners were easily brushed aside and by 1843 the key routes, which form a cross as the east–west and north–south lines meet in Brussels, had been completed. By then, Belgium, which was already heavily industrialized thanks to its extensive coal mines, had the densest network of railways in the world relative to its surface area. They were crucial in cementing the country together after the 1830 revolution, which led to Belgium's declaration of independence on 4 October that year. As the seminal history of the country states: 'Without the revolution, the railway would never have existed; without the railway the revolution would have been compromised.' [1]

Belgium, therefore, was the first country to be bound together by its railway system but many others, most notably Italy and Germany, used the iron road in the same way. Again, there is a

A watercolour celebrating the first train in Belgium, which ran from Brussels to Mechelen in May 1835.

symbiotic relationship between the railways and nationbuilding, in which it is difficult to separate out cause and effect. In the 1850s and 1860s, Italy – or rather the principalities into which it was still divided – was poor and largely rural and it had been slow to embrace the age of the train. There were barely 1,500 miles (2,400 km) of line by 1860, far fewer than in other Western European countries. The Second War of Independence, fought against the Austrian Empire in 1859, would kick off the process that resulted in the unification of Italy, but it would take until 1870 – and further conflict with Austria in 1866 – before unity was achieved. Improvement of the railways was a key policy for the new Kingdom of Italy from the outset, both to stimulate industrial development but also as a means of uniting the country. Despite a shortage of funds after the long series of wars, 1,200 miles (1,900 km) of new line were built in unified Italy's first five years of existence, making it possible for the first time to travel by rail between all the major cities of the peninsula except those in its sparsely populated south. Building the railway network was, as it had been in Belgium, a government-sponsored project. In another measure that demonstrated the importance the new nation attached to developing an effective transport system, the Italian railways were effectively nationalized as they were consolidated into four major companies that received subsidies from the state to provide a guaranteed rate of return for the shareholders. The centrality of the railways to the new but impoverished Italian state is neatly summed up by Susan Ashley, a historian of nineteenth-century Italian politics: 'The new government of united Italy could not afford to build and operate railroads, but nor could it afford not to.'[2]

In Germany – or rather Prussia, the dominant German state before the country's unification in 1871 – the creation of the railway network was driven much more directly by military imperatives. The Prussian army chief of staff, Helmuth von Moltke, widely recognized as a great strategist, was one of the

PREVIOUS PAGES Brindisi, Italy, 1866, a classic station building which would have accommodated a waiting room, a restaurant (possibly with two classes) and numerous other facilities.

first to understand the importance of railways to the conduct of war. As early as 1843, he wrote an article extolling their virtues as a weapon: 'Every new railway development is a military benefit, and for national defence it is far more profitable to spend a few million on completing our railways than on new fortresses.'[3] The British were also quick to grasp this. Following the Indian Mutiny – or Great Rebellion as it is known in India – in 1857, the government accelerated the railway building programme to make it easier and cheaper to move troops around the subcontinent to suppress unrest, rather than establishing large and expensive barracks in every major city.

In Prussia, the railways were organized systematically to prepare for conflict, especially with neighbouring France. The routing of new lines was often determined by the needs of the military, although the latter did not always win their battles with civil administrators and private railway companies who were keen to provide railways that were both socially useful and commercially viable. For example, military advisers were always pushing for railway lines to be built under the protection of fortresses – a rather quaint juxtaposition of medieval and modern military strategies – and trying to ensure that they were on the 'opposite' side of rivers or canals – that is, on the bank furthest from the likely invader, which may not have suited the commercial priorities of the railway. On military recommendations, numerous lines were constructed to strengthen the ability to move troops quickly westwards. In contrast with France, where the railways spread out, fan-like, from Paris, the German railway system was not centred on a particular city but, rather, was a network with good connections between most major conurbations. This would be of critical importance in both the Franco-Prussian War of 1870–1 and the First World War.

...

The building of the transcontinental lines in the US and in Canada can be seen as examples of nationbuilding and, more precisely, of consolidating a federal structure encompassing a vast geographical area. Until the Civil War of 1861–5, the US railways had been confined to the east of the country – partly because the immigrant population west of Chicago and St Louis remained small, but also because many of the western regions had not yet become part of the United States.

The building of the first transcontinental railway across the United States was a long time in gestation. First considered in the 1850s, at the time it was by far the most ambitious infrastructure project anywhere in the world. After years of debate, the Pacific Railway Acts were signed into law by President Lincoln in July 1862, during the Civil War. Their passage through Congress was facilitated by the absence of the Southern politicians whose states had seceded to form the Confederacy, and whose efforts to en-sure the transcontinental railway followed a route through their region had long delayed a political decision to proceed. As with many major railway projects, it took the efforts of one particularly obsessive, indeed fanatical, visionary to push the project through. Theodore Judah, a clergyman's son and experienced railway engi-neer who had helped build railway lines in both the east and west of the country, not only travelled to California to devise early versions of the route but, on returning to Washington, success-fully lobbied Congress and President Abraham Lincoln to push through the legislation with its generous funding arrangements.

Before the building of the Transcontinental Railway, the quickest route between America's west and east was to travel by ship from California southwards along the coast of Mexico to Central America, cross the Panamanian isthmus by land, and then pick up a boat again to complete the journey across the Caribbean to reach the eastern seaboard. The new railway linking coast to coast would open up the entire continent to development, transforming the US's manufacturing and economy, as well as enabling thousands to explore and settle their native lands to the west. Ironically, poor Judah Sadly, Judah would never see the line's completion as he died in November 1863, from a fever caught while making that long journey from coast to coast via Panama.

Construction of the line, which required 1,800 miles (2,900 km) of new railway to link existing lines in the east with the Californian coast, was allocated to two separate companies, the Union Pacific Railroad and Central Pacific Railroad. Oddly, despite its name, the latter, which turned its first shovelful of earth on 8 January 1863, was responsible for the western section starting from Sacramento in California, while the Union Pacific worked westwards from Council Bluffs in Iowa. In many respects the Transcontinental was a heroic enterprise, which reflected the new nation's pioneering spirit: despite having to cope with extreme weather conditions, difficult terrain in both mountains and desert and a shortage of labour, the navvies nonetheless managed to complete the task in just seven years. But the Transcontinental also laid bare some of the worst aspects of America's rapid development: many of the railroad company directors and managers enriched themselves through systematic corruption, and construction was dependent on the illegal appropriation of Native American land, breaking numerous treaties and promises. Moreover, this land grab did not just involve the route of the railway but also encompassed hundreds of thousands of acres allocated to the two companies as a way of subsidizing the project. Indeed, although the Transcontinental railroad was ostensibly a private enterprise, all its funding came from government sources – either directly through subsidy, which varied according to the difficulty of the terrain, or through generous grants of land.

The strangest aspect of this huge scheme is that no one set out clearly *why* it was being built and why it was worth spending

OVERLEAF A construction train of the Union Pacific Railroad, building the first transcontinental line across America, which opened in 1869.

RUCTION TRAIN 1868

millions of dollars of government funds to fund it. In some ways, the building of the Transcontinental was rather like climbing Everest or going to the South Pole, a challenge that simply demanded to be undertaken. Because the well-established technology of railway construction made it feasible to build the line, there was an imperative to do so. There were of course ostensible reasons, such as opening up markets to Asia and dealing with what settlers called the 'Indian Menace'. The most coherent motive, however, was the idea of 'opening up the West', providing access to the natural resources of a region that was seen, rather optimistically, as a land of plenty and whose exploitation was perceived to be part of America's destiny. The reality was rather different as the harsh climate and the lack of forests – and consequently wood for building houses and fences – meant the early settlers struggled to establish viable farms. The line would initially be little used after its completion in 1869, as it carried few passengers and there was not much call for haulage of freight.

While the motives behind the building of the line were rather vague, the effects of its completion would, however, eventually be far-reaching. By making it easier to access California and other western states, the Transcontinental would stimulate a massive shift westwards, both of people and economic activity – an enormously significant staging-post in the creation of the modern United States. Despite the early lack of traffic, several railway entrepreneurs saw the huge economic potential in accessing the west and soon other transcontinental lines were being built. Two of them, the Southern Pacific, which ran to Los Angeles, then a small town in southern California, and the Northern Pacific, which ended in Seattle, opened in 1883. By the end of the nineteenth century, there were no fewer than five transcontinental routes linking the midwest or the south to the Pacific. With the exception of the Great Northern Railway, built by a remarkable railway promoter, the one-eyed frontiersman James J. Hill, all these lines were stimulated by generous government grants of land. Soon the flow of immigrants, again helped by government intervention through subsidies and grants, ensured that the lines became well used.

The role played by this extraordinary enterprise in bringing America together retains great symbolism even today. The completion of the Transcontinental in 1869 is recognized as a turning point in American history. Promontory Point, Utah, the place where the railheads of the Union Pacific and Central Pacific met, has become something of a shrine and an expression of American unity. Sadly, Promontory Point is no longer on the line. In the early years of the twentieth century, Southern Pacific, which had taken over Central Pacific's operations in 1885, moved the route to a less sinuous – and consequently faster – alignment, bypassing Promontory entirely. The 150th anniversary, which occurred as this book was being written, was widely celebrated across the United States and marked by the issue of a set of stamps.* Oddly, the name 'transcontinental' is something of a misnomer as there has never been a regular direct coast-to-coast service† in the US because no single company ever controlled the entire route: services from the east generally ran to Chicago or St Louis, whence connecting western services departed.

...

Canada, then a British colony, was determined to emulate its southern neighbour by also building a transcontinental line.

---

* Indeed, as I was writing this section, I was contacted by *News-O-Matic*, a news service for school students read in schools across America, for an interview about the first Transcontinental.

† Apart from, briefly, between 1993 and 2005, when Amtrak ran its *Sunset Limited* service to Jacksonville, Florida, instead of New Orleans, because of the damage caused at the latter by Hurricane Katrina.

While commercial considerations such as the exploitation of minerals and the establishment of agriculture were a significant stimulus, nationbuilding was the most important consideration here too, since British Columbia, the westernmost province, was threatening secession. In the early 1870s, its rulers made the construction of a transcontinental line a precondition of joining the Dominion of Canada, rather than the United States, which had just acquired Alaska from Russia and would gladly have extended its new territory southwards. The building of the first Canadian transcontinental may not have attracted as much attention as the inaugural line south of the border, but as an engineering feat it more than matched its predecessor. Again, there was a massive personality behind the project – this time literally as well as figuratively. This was William Cornelius Van Horne, whose company, Canadian Pacific – including the name of the ocean was *de rigueur*, it seems, for all these early transcontinental railways – built the line. The Illinois-born Van Horne, a tubby, immensely powerful fellow wont to indulge in arm-wrestling contests with his navvies, worked all hours to complete the construction of the railway, which passed through far more difficult terrain than the American line. In order to stretch the 2,700 miles (4,345 km) from the developed region of Ontario through to the Pacific, the railway had to cross the Selkirk range of mountains in British Columbia as well as the Canadian Rockies. The workers had to endure weather conditions even worse than those further south when the first transcontinental had been built. Van Horne, who once fearlessly crossed a rickety trestle bridge over a 160-foot (50-m) ravine, despite having been advised not to, paid little heed to the safety and well-being of his workers, more than 800 of whom perished through want of basic safety measures. Owing to a number of delays caused by recurrent financial difficulties arising from higher than expected costs, the line was not completed until 1885, thirteen years after work on it had started.

It would be another thirty years before the second Canadian transcontinental was built. As its name implies, the Canadian Northern Railway took a more northerly route through the mountains. While the Canadian Pacific's main *raison d'être* was to bring the nation together, the motive behind the second line's construction was to attract settlers to the vast potential of the wheat fields of Saskatchewan and enable the harvested grain to be carried to the east. A third Canadian line, the Grand Trunk Pacific Railroad, was completed, rather unnecessarily, during the First World War, by which time a remarkable eight transcontinental railway lines stretched across North America. The tracks mostly survive today as important freight routes, boosted by trade with east Asia.

It is quite possible that without the construction of these railway lines across the North American continent, international boundaries would look very different today. There might well, for example, be a state called British Columbia (or rather Columbia) within the United States, or indeed a separate nation encompassing a huge coastline, like Chile, from the Mexican border to Alaska. And would the United States now have as many as fifty states?

...

A couple of decades after the completion of the first US transcontinental, Russia embarked on an even grander project to improve transport links with the most remote regions of its territory. The building of the Trans-Siberian Railway involved constructing a line to Vladivostok on the Pacific Ocean, a project that added almost 5,000 miles (8,000 km) of line to the country's existing rail network. Russia had been a relatively late entrant to the railway age and it had been slow to expand its network, which remained wholly inadequate for the needs of such a large country with a population density, in relation to its land area, just one-twentieth that of Britain. Combined with the fact that this huge nation had only just begun the process of industrialization, this made Russia an unlikely location for what was the most ambitious rail project in the world, requiring double the length of additional track required by the Canadian Pacific and three times that of the first transcontinental in the US.

As was the case with the other transcontinental lines, the motives behind the Trans-Siberian's construction were the subject of fierce debate, but broadly the principal driving forces were nationbuilding and expansionism. This time the major figure behind the line's construction was a former railway manager-turned-politician, Sergei Witte. As minister of finance from 1892, Witte saw the project as being of critical national importance and offering the prospect of enormous financial benefits in the long run, both for Siberia and for Russia as a whole. In promoting the project, which had been discussed for decades in government circles, Witte stressed what he saw as its advantages. The line could be used to transport grain, timber and minerals from a vast area, as well as providing a connection with the Pacific Ocean. More broadly, Witte perceived the railways as a catalyst for the faster development of the Russian economy. The building of the Trans-Siberian would stimulate the development of the heavy metallurgical industry for which the nation was blessed with huge resources. In turn, that economic development would help the Russian monarchy, in which Witte greatly believed, resist the forces of revolution that were always bubbling just below the surface. As a consequence, he argued, Russia, would be able take its place in the pantheon of great European nations like France and Great Britain, rather than being seen as an underdeveloped backwater.

Military considerations, however, were paramount. The completion of the Canadian transcontinental and the start of the Panama Canal project had raised fears among Russia's rulers that the country's territorial integrity was under threat. Tsar Alexander III, who made the ultimate decision to give the project the go-ahead, thought that as the railway would bring Siberia, a remote land into which most Russians never ventured, into the fold, it would make the nation's borders more secure. In a deliberately symbolic move, in 1890 he despatched his son – later Nicholas II, the last tsar – to Vladivostok, in Russia's far east, to lay the first ceremonial stone.

The military's support for the project was based not only on defensive considerations. The line would enable the Russian military better to defend Siberia against potential invaders from the south or from the ocean, but the military was also well aware that construction of the line afforded them the opportunity to expand Russian territory. Indeed, a treaty with a very weak China allowed the initial route of the Trans-Siberian to include a long section through Manchuria, an area of northeastern China, which saved some 600 miles (950 km) in length. However, Japan, the other major power in the region, regarded this development as a hostile act. Indeed, fears of encroachment on its sphere of influence in east Asia would lead Japan to launch a successful war against Russia in 1904–5.

Construction of the Trans-Siberian Railway, most of which was completed within a decade of the start of the work in 1891, was a remarkable feat. The difficulties faced by those who worked on the line were legion. Siberia is not only famously cold, but it was a vast barren territory with few inhabitants apart from exiles and a few nomadic tribespeople. The massive labour force of up to 80,000 men, which ultimately included convict labour, had to be recruited from western Russia and further afield, from places such as Persia (Iran) and even Italy. The line had to cross huge swathes of land without habitation or any natural resources that could be used in its building. The initial stages of construction, in western Siberia, were relatively easy, and finding a pass through the Ural

Mountains proved to be straightforward, but conditions became much more testing in the central section of the line, between the Ob river and Lake Baikal, where embankments had to be laid across swampy ground. With severe weather allowing work to be carried out for only about six months of the year, the difficulties at times seemed insuperable, but with unconstrained state funding and a very determined set of engineers, all the obstacles, logistic as well as geological and climatic, were overcome. In the east, the railway named after the Ussuri river was built too close to the fast-flowing torrent and had to be rebuilt, and heavy rains in what is the wettest part of Siberia caused further delays.

The Trans-Siberian Railway was opened in stages. The most difficult section, the Circum-Baikal railway through the hills around the southern coast of Lake Baikal, was not completed until October 1904 and only fully opened the following year. Until then, passengers had to transfer to a ferry or, in the winter when the lake froze over, horse-drawn sleds, to reach the other side of the lake.

The line was rather crudely built and in its early days witnessed many, mostly minor, accidents. After the Russo-Japanese War, however, there was considerable investment to transform the Trans-Siberian into a faster, safer and more efficient railway. The completion of the Circum-Baikal section, which involved 200 bridges and 33 tunnels, made it possible to run direct trains from Moscow to Vladivostok for the first time. The new line soon became very busy. By the end of the decade, a million settlers had been brought to Siberia, attracted by offers of free land and the establishment of a series of new towns and villages along the route. The government provided schools, churches and housing, and even made available a railway carriage that was kitted out as a mobile place of worship for the remotest regions where churches had not yet been built. Even today, most of the population of Siberia lives close to the tracks of the Trans-Siberian.

The railways not only stimulated the forging of strong states but also played a key role in the conflicts that resulted from their establishment. The first time that a railway played a major role in warfare was during the Crimean War, which broke out in 1854 and which pitted Britain, France and Ottoman Turkey against tsarist Russia. The British landed on the Crimean peninsula in the autumn of that year but were utterly unprepared for a war fought in freezing and wet conditions. The steep and winding road between the port of Balaklava where the ships landed and the besieged Russian naval port of Sebastopol was the sole supply route for the 30,000 troops. Hopelessly inadequate for the task the allies allotted to it, it soon – inevitably – became a permanent bottleneck.

The terrible conditions on the road, which greatly hampered the army's ability to fight, attracted considerable attention back in Britain as the Crimean War was one of the first conflicts to be the subject of detailed reports in the press accompanied by photographs. As a result, a group of railway engineers, led by Samuel Peto, a Whig MP who had built railways across the world, suggested that creating a railway between Balaklava and Sebastopol would greatly improve transport up to the site of the siege. The idea was quickly accepted by the government and a group of navvies was despatched 3,000 miles (4,800 km) from Britain to build the line. In just eight weeks, they constructed what was ambitiously called the Grand Crimean Central Railway, a ramshackle 7-mile-long (11 km) line powered by a combination of horses, locomotives, static engines, and, on its sloping section leading to the port, largely by gravity. Nevertheless, it did the trick. The line was completed by April 1855, and, thanks to the improved logistics which enabled extra supplies, large guns and men to be brought up rapidly to the siege, Sebastopol fell that September.

OVERLEAF The railways played a key role in the four-year-long American Civil War, during which nearly all the fighting took place near stations or junctions. The second Battle of Bull Run, in 1862, wrecked the nearby station at Manassas Junction.

While this episode helped military strategists understand that railways could play a key role in the logistics of conflicts, it was the American Civil War, fought between 1861 and 1865, which demonstrated unequivocally that the railways would change forever the way wars would be waged in the future. The 400 battles of the Civil War, effectively one for every four days of the four-year conflict, took place over an area the size of Europe. Many of these encounters were fought in sparsely populated localities, which was only possible because they could be accessed by rail. The railways' ability to move troops, matériel and supplies rapidly across long distances rendered the war bloodier, longer and more destructive than it would have been had it taken place a couple of decades previously. Throughout the Civil War, nearly all the crucial battles took place at railway junctions or near railheads.

The importance of the railways, which were far better developed in the North than the South – a key factor in the defeat of the Confederacy – was recognized from the outset by both sides. Abraham Lincoln was quick to bring the North's railways under government control, which was to give the Union side a decisive advantage. The Confederates' victory in the first major land battle of the war, at Bull Run in Virginia, in July 1861, 20 miles (32 km) southwest of Washington, DC, was achieved because fresh troops were brought to the battleground on a small but strategically important railway line, the Manassas Gap Railroad, which they then extended after the battle. The Confederates, however, made the mistake of not taking over their railway companies, which greatly hampered their logistics as the private companies that owned them drove a hard bargain.

Exercising direct control over their lines, the Federal government appointed Herman Haupt, a former superintendent of the Pennsylvania Railroad, to head up a new bureau created by the US War Department to construct and operate military railways as well as organize the repair of those damaged by the conflict.

Haupt, a graduate of West Point, the US military college, proved not only to be brilliant at building and rebuilding railroads but also set out clear rules for the operation of railways in conflicts. These included ensuring that railway personnel, rather than the military, ran the train services and set the timetable, and making sure that wagons were unloaded quickly and returned to depots so they could be reused: regulations that may seem obvious, but were to prove crucial in both the American Civil War and subsequent conflicts.

The construction and destruction of railways occupied much of the energy of the rival armies during the Civil War. If the South won the first battle of the Civil War thanks to the railways, the final sweep eastwards through the South from Chattanooga, Tennessee, to Atlanta, Georgia, by Union General William Sherman was only made feasible by the use of the railways as the key supply line. In his memoirs, Sherman recalled that without the railroads it would have been impossible to have conducted a campaign on the scale of his final assault on the South. Three different railroads created a 500-mile (800-km) supply line from Louisville, Kentucky, through to Atlanta, much of which was destroyed by his forces once he had advanced. Sherman, a meticulous fellow, later wrote: 'That single stem of railroad supplied an army of 100,000 men and 32,000 horses for the period of 196 days, from May 1 to November 19 1864.' He went on to compare what would have happened without the railway: 'To have delivered that amount of forage and food by ordinary wagons would have required 36,800 wagons, of six mules each ... a simple impossibility in such roads that existed in the region.'[4]

No wonder many European observers who witnessed the events of the Civil War went away to spread the message that railways were now the key weapon of war. Haupt's rules proved crucial to the successful operation of railways in both the Civil War and future conflicts over the next hundred years. Indeed, railways were to play a critical role in every significant conflict of the late nineteenth century, but it was in the First World War that their power and limitations would come to the fore. At the outbreak of war in August 1914, the railways were at their apogee, not just in terms of the size of the networks, but also because cars and lorries – and indeed the roads they ran upon – were still primitive affairs, so that railways were virtually the only efficient form of transport for both goods and people. In the half century since the American Civil War, there had been continuous expansion of all the major European rail networks and a growing recognition that their role in any future military conflict would be fundamental to a successful outcome. In Germany, in particular, they were the centrepiece of plans to mobilize for war. After his success in the Franco-Prussian conflict of 1870–1 in which railways had also played a crucial part, Otto von Bismarck – Chancellor of a unified German empire from 1871 – ensured that the state took over most of the private railway companies, so that he could deploy them to best effect when war broke out.

The Schlieffen Plan, first set out in 1905 and updated annually, was devised to demonstrate how the railways could be used to invade France and capture Paris within forty days, ensuring an early French surrender. The lines to the west were beefed up, but when the scheme was eventually activated in August 1914, greater than expected resistance on the part of the Belgians, the blowing-up of railway lines, dogged defence and then counter-attack by the French – supported by the British Expeditionary Force – meant that its key objective failed. And the stalemate that ensued on the Western Front, which lasted until the final stages of the war, was entirely a result of the logistics dominated by the railways. The swiftly dug trenches were supplied by mainline railways a few miles behind the lines where they were out of range of the guns, and then by 'field railways', little 60-centimetre-gauge (24 ins) lines that could easily be laid on fields that had been turned into battlegrounds. This efficient supply system was rather inflexible, but without adequate roads or much air power there was no alternative. The railways, therefore, were both the provider of mobility but also its main obstacle. They were, in sum, the essential determinant of the strategy of a war that was, until then, the bloodiest and most wide-ranging conflict in human history. It was fitting, therefore, that the armistice was signed in a railway carriage in the Forêt de Compiègne in November 1918.

# Robber Barons and Railway Cathedrals

As well as nationbuilding and playing a key role in war logistics, the railways were also crucial in moulding the future of capitalism. Not only were they a catalyst for economic changes on a massive scale, but the companies building and operating the lines soon became the biggest in their respective nations and, indeed, in the world.

Railways are natural monopolies: they require high levels of investment and the consolidation of different railway companies produces huge economies of scale. In Britain by 1844 a mere eleven companies already controlled half the rail network, while most of the others were tiny concerns running lines with an average length of just 12 miles (19 km). The railway mania of the 1840s, during which 4,600 miles (7,400 km) of line were built – roughly the total that received Parliamentary approval – led to further consolidation as the biggest companies used the capital generated from profits on their existing lines to invest in both expansion and the purchase of ailing rivals.

In order to control their burgeoning networks of routes, these large companies needed to embrace modern forms of organization and develop new skills. The unprecedented demands of running a railway required a more sophisticated form of management than was practised in other industries, both because of the sheer scale of their operations and, particularly, their geographical spread. As well as a head office to co-ordinate overall activity they had to employ large numbers of people away from base at stations, depots and locomotive sheds. Although communication between the various parts of the railway was made easier by the adoption of the telegraph in the 1850s, managing a workforce of several thousand people over a vast area remained a challenge. No contemporary business was so complex, nor employed such a large staff. At that time, manufacturing concerns were primarily individual factories. Only the army, the navy and the East India Company, a quasi-governmental organization that effectively ruled large parts of the Indian subcontinent, could compare in scale with the major rail companies emerging in the first twenty years of the advent of the iron road. The wide variety of assets such as stations, the rolling stock, the permanent way and the tunnels required management and maintenance, which in turn necessitated skilled workers and adaptable managers. Stations needed a host of booking clerks, ticket checkers and porters, and, of course, a station master to oversee them; depots, engineers and cleaners; head offices, timetable planners and operating staff; and trains, guards, drivers and firemen. That horrible term 'human resources' had not yet been devised, but, faced with such a veritable army of employees, the railway companies could have done with a more contemporary system of personnel management. In fact, the early companies leant heavily on military methods to manage their employees. The men – and they *were* all men in the decades up until the First World War, with the exception of a handful of female level crossing keepers – were provided with uniforms and were deemed to be 'railway servants', subject to a very strict hierarchy and discipline.

Even in these early days, it was recognized that safety of operations was an issue. As the railways became more crowded and the risk of collisions increased, the railways developed a system of learning from their mistakes, responding to accidents with both emergency and preventative measures. In truth, however, improvements in railway safety were introduced much too slowly. Until the last two decades of the nineteenth century, there was no legal requirement, either in Britain or the US, to introduce safety measures even when their need was all too apparent. The inevitable result was a considerable toll of deaths and injury on the railways, which we will look at in more detail in the next chapter. As was the case with the timetabling and co-ordinating of services, safety measures required skilled and effective management.

Although the principle of the joint-stock company with its limited liability, which meant that a company could go bust without taking down the directors with it, was established before the opening of the Liverpool & Manchester, it was the railway companies that made most use of the concept. With their huge appetite for capital, and their at times shaky finances, railways could not have developed without the protection of limited liability and it was their ready adoption of this corporate model that ensured its rapid spread. Since this new type of company structure developed from its use by the railway companies, it could be argued that every large limited liability commercial organization, both in Britain and elsewhere, is in fact a descendant of them.

In the decade after Britain's railway mania of the 1840s, the Great Western, the Midland and the Great Northern all continued to expand, but the behemoth of the period was the London & North Western Railway. This company, formed through the fusion of the London & Birmingham and the Grand Junction, and which made up the first 200 miles (320 km) of what is now the West Coast Main Line, prospered as it was the main route linking the capital with the two large and growing conurbations of Birmingham and Manchester.

The pioneer in terms of creating a more effective modern management system was Captain Mark Huish, the London & North Western's general manager from the company's formation in 1846 until 1858. Huish was both an able traffic manager – a vital new skill needed to run railways as they became busier – and an excellent negotiator in dealings with rival railway companies. A multi-talented man with a rather dictatorial style, he was able to make rapid and far-ranging decisions on both technical and operational matters. Most importantly, though, Huish introduced new forms of accountancy and management systems that were widely imitated across the rail industry and beyond.

A critical development was the separation of ownership from management. No longer would the owner or shareholders dictate company policy, which was now handed over to a new class of professional managers.

There was a tension between consolidation, which in effect meant the creation of ever-bigger monopolies, and competition, which was very much in line with the Victorians' fondness for free-market solutions. Yet, the fact remained that, as mentioned above, railways are a natural monopoly, requiring vast amounts of investment that can only be paid back through having exclusive access to a particular market. Therefore, while companies like the London & North Western and the Midland grew through mergers and acquisitions, the government was wary of allowing them to become too big and on several occasions rejected proposed mergers. It was not until after the First World War, and the Railways Act (or Grouping Act) of 1921, that the plethora of British railway companies, which had numbered a couple of hundred at the outset of the conflict, were forced by legislation to become the Big Four – the London & North Western, the London Midland & Scottish, the Great Western and the Southern. They operated for a quarter of a century until nationalization in 1948.

...

There was less concern in the US about the monopolistic nature of the companies that dominated the railway industry after the Civil War. Indeed, it was to counter the abuse of power of the huge rail companies that early anti-trust legislation was introduced in the late 1880s in the form of the Interstate Commerce Act. While several large railway companies in the east, such as the Baltimore & Ohio, the Pennsylvania and the Erie were well established before the Civil War, the biggest company to emerge in this early period was the carriage manufacturer and operator created by George Pullman. Pullman's name has become synonymous with sleeping-cars and, although he did not invent them, he ensured that his 'hotels on wheels', as they became known, were a byword for comfort and respectability. The radical aspect of Pullman's design was that the upper berth was suspended from the ceiling by ropes and pulleys, so that it could be stowed away in the daytime, allowing plenty of seating space for passengers. After the Civil War, Pullman's cars became more and more luxurious and he started providing copious and tasty meals in dining-cars. He became for a time the foremost industrial name in the United States, exporting the concept of the sleeping-car to Europe and Asia.

His factory near Chicago, the Pullman Palace Car Works, became so large that an entire eponymous town was developed, housing workers in pleasant and well laid-out surroundings but also constraining them, as they had to follow a whole set of rules and regulations. The inhabitants of Pullman were allowed to read only the company-produced and ever-cheery *Pullman News* rather than more widely circulated newspapers; goods could only be obtained from the company store; residents had to attend church on Sundays, and were expected to keep their houses in good order or face eviction. Pullman's legacy is marred by a bitter strike that took place in the early summer of 1894, just three years before his death, and which was triggered by the response of the newly formed American Railway Union and railroad workers to lay-offs and lock-outs. The dispute resulted in a quarter of a million railway employees across the country downing tools in sympathy and at least thirty railwaymen were killed in battles with the police and federal troops. It was a turning point in American labour history, spurring the formation of unions in other branches of industry. And such was the antagonism felt towards Pullman that, following his death in October 1897, he had to be buried in a lead-lined mahogany coffin which was then sealed inside a concrete block so that it could not be dug up by angry trade unionists.

The two companies that built the first Transcontinental, Union Pacific and Central Pacific, were at the time the biggest corporations in the country. As the American railway barons came to the fore in the last quarter of the nineteenth century, they melded together numerous rail companies to form further huge corporations. By the 1880s, the railway operators had become well-established businesses that were able to exploit their monopoly position on many routes. America was, by then, far ahead of Europe in terms of management and accounting practices, not least because of the sheer scale of its railway companies, which attracted awed respect and opprobrium in equal measure. While their size was indeed impressive, the lure of massive profits because of their monopolies meant that they also attracted unscrupulous entrepreneurs who did not always play by the rules or, indeed, stick to the law. A group of aggressive and ruthless businessmen emerged who became known as the railway barons or, for their opponents, the robber barons.

The first to come to prominence was Daniel Drew, a director of the Erie Railroad, in the northeastern US, a railway that was almost permanently in financial difficulties. In the 1860s Drew had made a fortune out of what would today be known as 'insider dealing'. It was, however, his titanic battle with the most famous of his rivals, Cornelius 'Commodore' Vanderbilt, that drew public attention to the activities of the barons. Vanderbilt had gained control of the New York Central Railroad which, like the Erie, ran between New York and Chicago, and it proved to be a cash cow as New York was booming and it was the line of preference for both people and freight heading upstate. However, Vanderbilt, like all these railway magnates, preferred to have a monopoly and so he wanted to take over the Erie. When Drew learnt of his rival's interest, he managed to print off large numbers of valueless share certificates and sold them to Vanderbilt who, on learning about the scam, promptly sued Drew and his two fellow directors, Jay

OVERLEAF Public dislike of the 'robber barons' who controlled American railroads was often portrayed in vivid illustrations like this one from *Puck* magazine, showing 'The protectors of our industries' crushing the workers.

Gould and Jim Fisk. There followed perhaps the most bizarre episode in American railroad history, when the three shysters fled to New Jersey, where they had immunity from New York's judicial system, and holed up in a hotel with a large swathe of cash. Vanderbilt, rather surprisingly, lost the case when it eventually reached the courts, but it is not the convoluted details of this highly publicized episode that are important but rather the lasting impression of the railway it created in the public mind.

Gould was another of the notable railway magnates to make his mark during this 'Gilded Age' of rapid economic growth and rampant speculation. He ran the Erie Railroad for several years from 1868, but, after being ousted in a shareholders' coup, apparently went straight and headed west. There, taking advantage of depressed stock prices arising from an economic depression – the so-called Panic of 1873 – Gould took control of the Union Pacific. He went on to build up another empire of more than 10,000 miles (16,093 km) of track, which at the time represented one-seventh of the whole country's rail network.

It was the dream of several of these moguls to control a network of lines across the whole of the United States and run coast-to-coast services, but none were successful in that aspiration. The one who came closest and who managed to amass the largest ever network was Edward Harriman. A clergyman's son who had left school at fourteen to work as a messenger boy on Wall Street, Harriman already owned the Illinois Central when the stock market panic of 1893 and the subsequent recession led to a quarter of America's 364 railroads going bust. Harriman picked up a lot of these lines, including the massive Union Pacific, for a song and turned them into money spinners. By the early 1900s, he controlled more track miles – 25,000 miles (40,000 km) – than any previous magnate, but, like the other railroad barons, he attracted widespread opprobrium for his dubious business methods.

This universal dislike of the barons was not always merited. Several, in fact, built up efficient railway systems that provided good transport links for their passengers. However, the public antagonism towards the barons came from three sources: dislike of their monopoly status; criticism of the methods they used to accumulate their empires, particularly in their early days; and distaste for the fact that they were not only ruthless, pugnacious and extremely rich but all too ready to show off their wealth, often, for example, hitching their opulent private carriages to ordinary service trains. Cornelius Vanderbilt's colossally wealthy eldest son, William Henry Vanderbilt, when questioned about the scrapping of a popular train service, was quoted as responding: 'The public be damned!' Although it is unclear whether Vanderbilt Jr actually uttered these words, the widespread belief that he did, proved to be very damaging to the reputation of the big railway magnates.

...

In the more highly regulated environment of Europe, there was less scope for such entrepreneurs to emerge. The biggest railway empire of the late nineteenth century was that of the Rothschild bank, based in Paris, which built up a remarkable collection of mostly cross-frontier railways, including the Südbahn in Austria, the Chemins de Fer du Nord and the Paris–Lyon–Mediterranée in France, as well as various other lines in Europe. The Rothschilds even funded the building of the Bengal Nagpur Railway in India. This dominance was not always welcomed, and indeed the new government of the recently unified Italy prevented them from expanding their empire there in the 1870s by banning foreign capital from taking over the railways.

Nonetheless, the railways' consolidating tendencies and hunger for capital created an irresistible trend towards the dominance of the industry by ever-bigger companies. That process accelerated in the second half of the nineteenth century, when the most visible expression of the size and power of the railway companies were the stations in the centres of major cities. In the first days of the railways, no one had given much thought to stations and they were crude affairs, little more than a small building housing a ticket office, possibly a waiting-room and boarding points, which initially might have been merely a step up to reach the train rather than a platform. In the US, where newly built railways tended to be greatly undercapitalized, often an inn or general store would serve as the ticket office.

Within a couple of decades, though, as the vast monolithic companies started to emerge, great termini, designed with little consideration of expense or modesty, were being erected in city centres, in tandem with the spread of the iron road. Not surprisingly, it was in imperial Britain that the first station with claims to grandeur was completed, when Euston, just a mile or so north of the centre of London, was chosen as the terminus for the London & Birmingham Railway. From its opening in 1837, it boasted a 200-foot (610-m) engine shed and, most ostentatiously, a 70-foot (21-m) arch with Doric columns that served no purpose other than to inspire awe. Even better, a decade later, when Euston became the headquarters of the much larger London & North Western Railway, the neo-classical Great Hall with its double staircase and coffered ceiling designed by the architect Philip Hardwick was added.*

The idea of the cathedral-like station soon spread to France, where the Gare de l'Est in Paris – the western terminus of the Paris–Strasbourg and Paris–Mulhouse railways – was completed in 1849. Thanks to the huge semi-circular window that overlooks the entrance, the Gare de l'Est was considered the most stylish

---

* Sadly, both the Hall and the arch were demolished in the 1960s, when the station was rebuilt.

station of the age. Competition between the various railway companies in Paris and London accounts for the fact that both cities have numerous termini, sometimes within sight of one another. The Gare de l'Est is a stone's throw from the Gare du Nord in Paris's 10th arrondissement, while the hugely contrasting stations of King's Cross, with its clean Italianate lines, and the neo-Gothic St Pancras, are adjacent to one another on London's Euston Road.

The station frontages, many of which housed large hotels, were matched in grandeur by the inelegantly named 'sheds' behind them, which provided cover for passengers and, rather less helpfully, retained the smoke from the engines. Grandest of all was William Barlow's amazing structure at St Pancras, which is more than 218 yards (200 m) long and 82 yards (75 m) wide, and was, at the time of its completion in 1868, the longest such span anywhere in the world.

One of the side effects of the affluence of the railway companies that built these new stations was that their large profits enabled them to experiment with all kinds of styles, irrespective of cost. Indeed, the very word 'eclectic' could have been coined specifically to describe this collection of buildings, most of which fortunately survive today as a continuing reminder of the railways' early heyday. In the words of one writer on the cultural impact of the railways: 'At its most basic level, the railway station was the nineteenth century's distinctive contribution to architectural forms. It combined within itself in eloquent reflection of the age which produced it both a daring and innovative modernity and a heroic and comforting traditionalism.'[1]

It was not only in major cities that grand, even opulent, railway stations were built. The Union station in St Louis, Missouri, offers a classic example of the ambition and range of architectural styles of the late-nineteenth-century railway station. Designed by the German-born architect Theodore Link for the Terminal Railroad

OVERLEAF The magnificent Gare de l'Est in Paris, built in the neo-classical style, was opened in 1849 but was later extended. It is pictured here in 1880.

Association of St Louis, it was built to serve all the twenty-two railroads – the most served by any station in the world – in the region. Completed after two years of construction in 1894, Union station boasted – in addition to its ticketing offices and passenger waiting-rooms – a hotel, restaurant, a Grand Hall decorated with gold leaf, a barrel-vaulted ceiling, Romanesque arches and 280-foot (85-m) clock tower. One writer described the style in which it was built as 'Romanesque Norman Revival and Chateau'.[2] The station was soon expanded to become the centrepiece of the St Louis World's Fair, held in 1904.

Large stations were designed to attract attention and to represent the power of the railway companies, but also – with their waiting-rooms, cafés and ever-helpful porters – to offer a welcoming environment. There is an inherent contradiction here. Arrive in any unfamiliar town and the experienced traveller will immediately be able to recognize the local station with its bustling passengers, its hordes of hustlers and its line of attendant taxis waiting for business, and yet the diversity of styles of stations is almost infinite. There was no blueprint and few rules other than to provide tracks and platforms, ticket halls and refreshments.

In America, the pre-Civil War railroads, ever short of capital, were slow to imitate their European counterparts. It was not really until the last quarter of the nineteenth century that imposing railway stations began to appear. The railroads – or combinations of several neighbouring companies brought together by civic authorities – made up for lost time by building stations that were grander, larger and better designed than their European equivalents. The masterpiece of US railway station architecture was undoubtedly Grand Central station in New York City. Its train shed, built by Cornelius Vanderbilt in the early 1870s as part of Grand Central Depot, the original station on the site, was based on Barlow's in St Pancras. The station went through various

PREVIOUS PAGES The iron latticed arched roof of St Pancras station, which opened in 1869, was designed by William Barlow and spanned 140 feet, the largest such structure in the world at the time.

reconstructions in the early twentieth century, but the train shed survives to this day as part of the entirely renovated station.

The heyday of the American railway station was in the early twentieth century when mergers and joint working arrangements resulted in the construction of a series of 'union' stations where rival or newly merged railroads could share facilities and allow passengers to change trains more easily, a model that had become well established in Europe half a century previously. Union station in the US capital, Washington, DC, is probably the best-known example, with its triumphal arch entrance, grand high-ceilinged lobby and its neo-classical style leavened with a hint of modernism. Outside the eastern seaboard, the largest of these massive structures was the station on the Missouri side of Kansas City, whose Beaux-Arts style would not be unfamiliar to a Parisian taxi driver. Completed in 1914, it housed services from a dozen railroad companies. Today it is used by just three Amtrak trains per day serving 421 daily passengers, compared with 670,000 at its peak in 1945, although its vast unused offices have been refurbished as a 'Science City'. If anywhere reflects the decline of passenger services in the US, it is Kansas City.

While most European stations have survived to see the twenty-first century, with the exception, as we have seen, of the original Euston in London and a few unlucky ones dotted around the continent that succumbed to war damage, the US has seen rather more acts of railway architecture vandalism, prompted, at times, by a desire to bury its railway heritage in these car-obsessed times. An early casualty was Park Square in Boston, Massachusetts, which was completed in the 1870s with a reading room and a billiard hall as well as a waiting area decorated with rose windows and clusters of gaslights, but then torn down in the dying days of the nineteenth century. It was replaced by the pleasant, but far less remarkable, Boston South station, which for a time just before the First World War became the busiest railway station in the world. However, there is no doubt that the most grievous piece of railway destruction carried out in the US – and indeed possibly anywhere in the world – was of the supremely elegant Pennsylvania station, fronted by a Doric colonnade modelled on the Acropolis. The exterior was demolished in 1963, just fifty-three years after its completion, as rail passenger numbers declined. The below-ground elements, including concourses and waiting-rooms, were retained under the office block and Madison Square gardens sports centre that replaced the glorious station. Today, paradoxically, it has once again become a very busy station, but passengers now have to negotiate a series of crowded underground corridors with low ceilings and narrow passages that are wholly inadequate.

Fortunately, though, the vast majority of the great stations built across the world in the heyday of the railways have survived – a lasting homage to the greatest invention of the nineteenth century. With the rediscovery of the railways in the twenty-first century, some of these venerable stations have been revived and refreshed (as happened in London with the refurbishment of St Pancras, once threatened with demolition, as the Eurostar terminal) or, in the case of stations as diverse as the Gare d'Orsay in Paris and Manchester Central, repurposed (as a museum and a conference centre respectively).

...

Just as the railway companies were the first big corporations to emerge as the Industrial Revolution created the modern capitalist economy, so the forces of labour began to fight back against the might of these corporations. It was not unexpected, therefore, that the strongest of the early trade unions represented railway workers. In Britain, after several early attempts to create railway unions, the Amalgamated Society of Railway Servants

(ASRS), the precursor of today's RMT (the National Union of Rail, Maritime and Transport Workers), was founded at Derby in 1871 in response to the mounting toll of deaths and serious injuries to railway workers. On average, the railways killed 682 workers every year during the 1870s, and most of the victims received scant, if any, compensation. While safety was the core of the union's campaigning efforts, it soon addressed more general issues of pay and conditions, particular the eight-hour working day. Train drivers, however, did not join the ASRS but instead formed a separate union that became, in 1880, the Associated Society of Locomotive Steam Enginemen and Firemen (ASLEF), a division that still exists today. After numerous strikes and other forms of industrial action over ensuing decades, the unions managed to change working conditions in the industry for the better and established good terms of pay and conditions for their members. Safety for workforces improved dramatically, thanks to innovations such as automatic coupling, but even as recently as the 1980s, it was not unusual for as many as thirty railway workers to be killed while carrying out their duties in the course of a single year. In the twenty-first century, with the introduction of hi-vis clothing and safety fencing and many more line closures, deaths of railway employees have – happily – become very infrequent events.

In the US, too, strong unions emerged from the railways. The pattern mirrored that of the UK. In the 1860s, a few local 'brotherhoods' emerged but in the ensuing couple of decades they coalesced into effective unions able to challenge intransigent managements and win better working conditions and higher wages for their members. The railway companies were reluctant to recognize them at first, but gradually the new breed of professional managers, who were at one remove from the owners, realized that accepting the existence of unions was inevitable. Over time the tide turned and, from a position of non-recognition, the

OVERLEAF The magnificent Pennsylvania station in New York, completed in 1910, was demolished in the 1960s in what has been called one of the worst acts of architectural vandalism of the twentieth century.

major railroads found themselves unable to resist many union demands. In addition to the Pullman lock-out, there were two other major strikes in the final quarter of the nineteenth century, the Great Railroad Strike of 1877, triggered by wage cuts by the Baltimore & Ohio, and the Great Southwest Railroad Strike of 1886 against Jay Gould's Union Pacific and Missouri Pacific railroads. The net effect of these three prolonged disputes was to ensure that in the twentieth century managements across the railroad industry had to take into account workers' views when making decisions. Indeed, the railroad unions remain a powerful force in the industry today.

Apart from the labour unions, the best-organized critics of the US railroads were the farmers. The railways had changed the nature of American farming. No longer could farmers simply take their produce by horse and cart to the local market. The larger farms that were established on huge tracts of land sold by the railways at knockdown prices required rail transport for their produce as they were producing cash crops for a much bigger market. Farmers had no alternative but to use the services of the local railroad company, which inevitably had a monopoly and set the freight rates, and understandably they came to regard the costs of transportation as an unavoidable and burdensome tax. Although initially the railways seemed to understand this and charged preferential rates, gradually the cost of transport increased and farmers began to take a more hostile attitude towards the railroad companies on whom they depended. Why, in particular, they asked, did it cost more per mile to send produce over short distances than long ones? There were good reasons for this, in fact, such as the cost of loading and unloading, but they fell on deaf ears. Soon a huge organization, known as The Grange, with 800,000 members at its peak, was established to articulate farmers' complaints against the railroads. These are set out in *The Octopus*, a bestselling novel by Frank Norris, published in 1901, which centres on the conflict between Californian wheat farmers and a railroad company, and which describes the railroad as 'that great monster, iron-hearted, relentless, infinitely powerful'.

To some extent this is unfair, as the railroads were, mostly, conscious of the farmers' needs, but The Grange's grievances alongside tales of 'evil' robber barons saw hostility towards the railroad companies build to a crescendo towards the end of the nineteenth century. This public attitude to the railways and their bosses would not be so important had it not led, in the early twentieth century, to strong regulation of the American railroad companies. While some of those regulations were undoubtedly necessary to restrict their exploitation of their monopoly status, in later years, particularly after the Second World War, they would prevent the American railroads from acting flexibly in the face of growing competition from motor vehicles and aviation.

# A Safer and
# Better Journey

Early trains were uncomfortable affairs and little thought was given to passenger comfort. In Britain, third-class accommodation on some lines – notably the Great Western, which ran its first trains in 1838 – consisted of open-top wagons with no shelter whatsoever and hard benches for a lucky few. A bad accident in 1841, in which nine passengers were killed after the train hit a landslide at Sonning cutting, near Reading in Berkshire, put paid to that most uncomfortable method of travel. Right from the beginning, there were three classes on the British railways with very different standards of comfort – wooden benches in cramped compartments in third class in contrast to comfortable upholstered seats with far more room for passengers to stretch their legs in first class and reasonable comfort in second. The railways were in many ways a social leveller and a liberating force, since they enabled people of relatively modest means to travel around the country. But by imposing a system of classification – which had not really existed in previous methods of transport, such as stagecoaches – they reinforced the strictly observed social divisions of early Victorian Britain.

Quite apart from their distinctive locomotive technology, the railways in the US were different in many other respects. The companies building the early American railroads were always short of capital and, given that the lines tended to be far longer than those in Europe, it was imperative for them to keep costs down. The average construction cost per mile was thus around one-fifth of the level in Britain. Cheapness, though, came at a price as both the quality of the railroad infrastructure and conditions for passengers were much inferior. American lines had considerably sharper curves, relatively steep gradients and a lower standard of track, which gave an uncomfortable ride. Bridges were flimsy affairs made of wood or sometimes even non-existent, with passengers having to transfer to a ferry. Drainage was poor, leading to flooding, and stations were small simple wooden structures with no facilities. The authors of *The Encyclopedia of North American Railroads* are remarkably candid about the inferiority of US lines in comparison with British ones:

> It was very different in Britain. The homeland of the railway was a very rich nation and could afford to do everything on a first-class basis. Its lines were models of civil engineering, built with gentle grades and broad curves. They crossed streams on great masonry viaducts such as the Romans would have built. Its stations were palaces with great high ceilings encased in costly stone.[1]

There is an element of 'the grass is greener on the other side' and even romanticizing here. The first British railways were indeed built to a higher standard than those across the Atlantic, but they were also pretty basic, as were the early stations, which were little more than sheds from which a few tracks emerged. The railways made quicker progress in Britain, however, in their early years at least. The railway mania of the 1840s, with its huge increase in route mileage, resulted in many technological improvements: locomotives got bigger, tracks more reliable, signalling systems more sophisticated and tunnelling became routine. Rather more slowly, and mostly after the Civil War, America, too, saw major improvements to its railways. For example, the locomotives of the 1830s had perhaps four or six wheels, weighed at most around 10 tons and could haul at best 200 tons on a level track. Twenty years later, weighing perhaps up to 20 tons and with twice as many wheels, they were able to haul loads of up to 500 tons.

On both sides of the Atlantic, first-class passengers enjoyed benefits such as picnic baskets, blankets for long night-time journeys and steam heating. However, the vast majority of travellers used third-class coaches, where improvements were slow to arrive. Standards varied considerably from company to company. Those that were prospering were able to offer the best facilities, while the strugglers scrimped to save money. As in America, the big companies in Britain also attracted the harshest censure, as they were seen as rapacious monopolies or, worse, fraudsters who had cost many middle-class investors their hard-earned savings during the railway mania. Many acquired imaginative but unwanted nicknames based on their acronyms, so the Manchester, Sheffield & Lincolnshire became the Mucky, Slow & Lazy while the Oxford, Worcester & Wolverhampton was known as 'Old Worse and Worse'.

The most damaging criticism of the railway companies was that the railways were dangerous. As we have seen, in the very early days of train travel, the infrequency of trains and their slowness meant there were few major accidents, but in the second half of the nineteenth century, accidents became a regular feature on railways across Europe and the US, with collisions, bridge failures, signalling errors and derailments.

The complaints levelled at the railways were entirely justified. A callous attitude, perhaps best summed up as 'accidents will happen and there is nothing we can do about it', appears to have prevailed in the minds of railways' owners. It was undoubtedly born of their pressing need to maximize profits and keep costs down to a minimum in order to satisfy their shareholders. Nothing characterizes this complete disregard for safety better than the fact that ticket inspectors on the first passenger lines had to move from compartment to compartment by walking perilously along an externally fitted wooden board. Fortunately this practice did not last long, and a new system whereby trains stopped at special sites near the end of the journey for tickets to be inspected was introduced on several early long-distance routes.

On both sides of the Atlantic, the second half of the nineteenth century witnessed a series of spectacular rail accidents which attracted widespread press interest and opprobrium in equal measure. In Britain, the involvement of Charles Dickens, by then an internationally famous author, in a rail disaster and his readiness to campaign on the issue undoubtedly added to the public clamour for improved safety. Dickens, along with his mistress and her mother, was a passenger on a train that derailed at Staplehurst in Kent in June 1865 because track-workers, misinformed about the schedule, had removed a rail. It was, in the novelist's own words, a 'terribly destructive accident',* killing ten people and injuring forty, and it left Dickens deeply traumatized. Railroad accidents in the US often exacted a heavier toll. A collision between two trains at Whitemarsh Township, Pennsylvania, in July 1856, killed as many as sixty. Its status as the world's greatest railway disaster up to that date earned it the name 'The Great Train Wreck of 1856'.

Bridge failures were a particularly common cause of accidents in the aftermath of the Civil War, when both the US economy and rail network were expanding rapidly. Trains had become heavier, putting extra stress on the many bridges over creeks and rivers which had often been built on the cheap, using inadequate and, crucially, under-engineered designs. The worst of these accidents was the Ashtabula river disaster in December 1876, when a Lake Shore & Michigan Southern service plunged into a river following a bridge failure. The death toll of ninety-two included a well-known gospel singer, Philip Bliss, which increased public interest in what was the worst rail accident in nineteenth-century US history.

In the UK, where bridges were generally more modest affairs because of the relatively gentle nature of the terrain, failures were less commonplace. However, one of Britain's most infamous disasters did involve a bridge weakness and occurred just three

---

* Dickens's description comes from the postscript to his novel *Our Mutual Friend*, the manuscript of which he was carrying with him on the train when the disaster took place.

OVERLEAF An engraving depicting the bridge collapse of December 1876 at Ashtabula on the Lake Shore Railroad, Ohio. Rail disasters such as this were commonplace in the nineteenth century.

years after the Ashtabula accident, in December 1879. All seventy-five people aboard a train crossing the Tay at Dundee in Scotland, at the time the world's longest bridge, perished following the collapse of the central span during a storm. The fault lay with the design, which had not ensured that the bridge was sufficiently robust to withstand weather of that magnitude, even though this was relatively commonplace on Scotland's east coast.

Both these disasters contributed to improvements in rail safety. In the US, as the authors of the *The Encyclopedia of American Railroads* put it, 'by the 1880s bridge failures had become an expensive embarrassment and reform was in the air'.[2] Railroad companies now called upon engineers to produce improved designs and state legislatures initiated more rigorous inspection

regimes. In the UK, the result was the stunning and lasting glory of the Forth bridge, which opened in 1890 and is perhaps the most famous railway bridge in the world. If it appears rather over-engineered, that is because Thomas Bouch, the designer of the Tay bridge, was sacked as its engineer and his idea for a suspension bridge was replaced by a magnificent cantilever bridge, designed to tolerate higher levels of wind resistance than originally envisaged.

Bridge collapses were not the only causes of railway accidents. Collisions, in particular, became more frequent as

The Tay bridge disaster, when a train plunged into the river on a stormy night in December 1879, was caused by poor engineering and led to many improvements.

the tracks became busier. Every extra train on the network added risk, especially as signalling systems were still crude and unreliable. This was particularly the case in the US, where trains were still despatched on the timetable and train-order system. Essentially, this meant allowing trains to depart at pre-set intervals and relying on the expectation that if a train broke down unexpectedly, a flagman would run down the track to alert any subsequent service. Inevitably, that procedure occasionally broke down. While the telegraph, by then in universal use, could be called upon at times to prevent accidents, there was no way to communicate with a train once it was on the move, which meant that errors leading to potential head-on disasters could not be rectified. And the potential causes of disaster were many and various: inexperienced rail staff, a misread train order, an unusual extra service such as a holiday special and, worst of all, the fact that sometimes a blind eye was turned towards drivers who, running late on single track lines, ignored the scheduled meeting point at a particular crossing-point where there were two tracks and consequently put the train at risk of a head-on collision.

This catalogue of disasters demonstrates that there was remarkably little external oversight of the industry for much of the nineteenth century. In Europe, there was some early legislation with, for example, the involvement of the British Board of Trade in the investigation of accidents, but by and large the industry was self-policing. In the US a few states created bodies with some responsibility for inspecting railways, but it was not until the 1870s that this began to become the norm. Remarkably, it was not until 1901 that railway companies were required by law to report accidents to the government. Improving safety on the railways was generally a matter of learning from experience so reporting was very important, and even before this legislation, improvements had begun to be made.

The increasing number of railway accidents in the second half of the nineteenth century led to increasing criticism of the railway companies and their failure to invest in safety features, as this September 1874 print from *Punch* shows.

# RAILWAY RESPONSIBILITY.

Mr. Punch. "NO, NO, MR. DIRECTOR, *THEY'RE* NOT SO MUCH TO BLAME. IT'S *YOUR* PRECIOUS FALSE ECONOMY, UNPUNCTUALITY, AND GENERAL WANT OF SYSTEM THAT DOES ALL THE MISCHIEF."

In Britain, the strategy to prevent collisions was more sophisticated than in the US, as it relied on a system of creating 'blocks' of track which were controlled by the signalling system in order to prevent two trains being in the same block at any point. The system was greatly improved after the June 1889 Armagh rail disaster, in Ireland, in which eighty people were killed and three times that number injured, most of whom were schoolchildren on a Sunday School outing. The very heavily laden train carrying the children had to mount a steep incline, but the locomotive lacked sufficient power and the train stalled. The train crew decided to divide the train and take forward the front portion, leaving the rear portion on the running line. However, because this part of the train was not independently braked, it ran back down the slope and collided with a following train, with tragic results.

The accident at Armagh highlighted several shortcomings, most notably the fact that the train did not have automatic brakes which failed safe if the system malfunctioned. As well as being, at the time, Europe's worst railway disaster, Armagh was the most significant accident in British rail history, in that it resulted in the introduction of much more stringent legislation. According to L. T. C. Rolt, eloquent author of the most famous treatise on railway accidents, *Red for Danger*, 'in those shattered coaches of the ill-fated excursion train, the old happy-go-lucky days of railway working came to their ultimate end and the modern phase of railway working began.'[3] The Regulation of Railways Act (1889), introduced less than three months after the Armagh collision, mandated a system that survives to this day, known as 'lock, block and brake'. *Interlocking* to ensure that the aspect of the signals corresponds to the way that the track points are set; *block*, by which the track is divided into sections into which only one train can enter; and *brake*, the provision of a fail-safe system of continuous brakes throughout the train. In the words of the act, 'the brake must be instantaneous in action, and capable of being applied by the engine-driver and guards ... to every vehicle of the train, whether carrying passengers or not'.

In the US, a federal body known as the Interstate Commerce Commission, created in 1887 by the Interstate Commerce Act, took an increasingly active role in safety regulation. Jurisdiction over matters of rail safety passed to the Commission from the individual states and it began to investigate the causes of accidents. Thanks to this more interventionist regime, the rate of accidents on what was a fast growing railway declined sharply.

While the increased scrutiny of rail safety reduced the rate of accidents in terms of deaths per million passenger miles, there were still several disasters with fatalities in three figures. This was especially the case during the First World War when the railways were overused and maintenance scaled back, and there were major incidents in Britain, France, Romania and the US, with death tolls in the hundreds. A train crash at Ciurea, in Romania, in January 1917, may have killed more than 1,000, while the derailment of a troop train at Saint-Michel-de-Maurienne in Savoie in southeastern France in December of the same year caused a fire in which at least 650 people lost their lives. However, as we will see in the final chapter, large-scale train crashes have become increasingly rare across the world in recent years, thanks to technological developments and more rigorous inspection and monitoring.

...

As well as enhanced levels of safety, passengers in the final quarter of the nineteenth century began to enjoy a much better general experience of the railways. In Britain, the introduction of corridors and vestibules, enabling people to move from one carriage to another during the journey, was a significant step forward in passenger comfort, not least because it enabled them to go to the toilet. There were no on-board facilities for early railway travellers and long-distance trains routinely stopped at pre-planned destinations to provide 'comfort breaks' for passengers. It was not unknown, though, for passengers to bring their own devices with local shops near stations selling "'travelling conveniences'" for wearing under everyday dress'[4] that were made of rubber and strapped to the leg. While men could, in extremis, open their compartment door, women were more constrained. But they also improvised by taking on board large baskets in which a pot could be hidden, and the long dresses that were worn at the time could provide suitable cover for those who might have difficulty holding out for the duration of the journey. Toilets appeared on trains only very slowly from the 1850s onwards, and it was not until the end of the century, when corridor trains in Britain became commonplace, that travellers could be more or less guaranteed to find facilities on board. In this respect, as we have seen, the trains in the US were ahead of those in Europe, on-board toilets being provided for long-distance passengers almost from the outset.

Providing food for passengers while on the move was even slower to arrive. In Britain, the first to enjoy meals on the trains

George Pullman designed his first luxury Sleeping Car in 1865 and his name became synonymous with premium train travel.

were passengers from Derby, in 1875, who were offered luncheon baskets by the Midland Railway, but the big innovation was the restaurant car, provided for the first time courtesy of that great innovator George Pullman in 1879. Travellers on the Great Northern's services between King's Cross and Leeds could pay a supplement to sit in the restaurant car, where they would be served at table from an on-board kitchen where the meals, which of course cost extra, were prepared. Despite this apparent great leap forward in comfort, at the time most passengers were still accommodated in compartments without any connection between them. It was not until 1893 that the first corridor trains were introduced. Deployed first on services between London and Scotland, the trains were equipped with vestibules connecting all the carriages, allowing passengers of all classes to make use of the restaurant cars during what were, at the time, journeys of at least seven hours.

In the US, the Baltimore & Ohio experimented with dining-cars in the late 1840s but the idea did not take on. For many years American trains, which typically made far longer journeys than those in Europe, stopped at stations where restaurants provided meals, though usually of very poor quality. In the 1870s, an entrepreneur named Fred Harvey set out to provide a better service for the Santa Fe railroad by opening a series of diners along the route, which ran southwest into New Mexico from Kansas and through to California. 'Harvey Houses' undoubtedly provided more wholesome food than had previously been available, but they were also famous for their employment of waitresses, dubbed the 'Harvey Girls', to serve the customers.

This was a pioneering move, not just in staffing the restaurants, but in also helping to bring young, single – and utterly respectable – women to the southwest, which had previously offered very few possibilities of marriage to the young immigrants working on its farms and ranches. Such was their fame that the Harvey Girls were the subject of an eponymous 1944 musical film starring Judy Garland.

The US railroads were also quicker off the mark with the introduction of sleeper trains. As soon as longer journeys were established, and trains were able to run at night, the companies provided blankets or a pillow to help passengers sleep. The first purpose-built sleeping-cars were brought into service in 1843 by the New York & Erie Rail Road. Beds had to be made up with the help of iron rods between facing seats but passengers complained the horsehair cushions were so scratchy that sleep was all but impossible.

Again, Pullman was the innovator. He first converted two cars of the Chicago & Alton Railroad in 1859 to provide the upper and lower berths that are so familiar to sleeper car travellers across the world today. His efforts to spread the innovation were interrupted by the Civil War, but after the conflict ended and the transcontinental lines were completed, Pullman cars began to appear on trains across the country, gradually becoming more comfortable and capable of accommodating more passengers. Pullman's coaches were open plan: passengers slept in berths parallel to the tracks, with only curtains to provide any privacy. The sleepers were introduced in Europe, but the Compagnie Internationale des Wagon-Lits, founded in 1874 by the Belgian entrepreneur George Nagelmackers, soon emerged as the main provider of sleeping-cars on this side of the Atlantic. Unlike Pullman's cars, which were open plan, the Wagon-Lits carriages were divided into compartments and passengers slept at right angles to the direction of travel, a design which seemed better to suit European tastes. They were a huge success and Nagelmackers developed a network of sleeper services that ran across numerous countries in Europe including, most famously, the *Orient Express*, which first ran in 1883 linking Constantinople (Istanbul) with Paris via Bucharest, Budapest and Vienna.

The Orient Express took passengers across the whole of eastern Europe, linking Paris with Constantinople (now Istanbul) for more than a century after opening in 1883, but its trains were never the scene of a murder.

# C<sup>ie</sup> WAGONS LITS

# The GOLDEN ARROW
## ALL PULLMAN TRAIN
### DAILY BETWEEN
# LONDON   CALAIS   PARIS
*Departs*: LONDON  10.45 a.m.  *Arrives*: PARIS  5.40 p.m.
*Departs*: PARIS  12 noon  *Arrives*: LONDON  7.15 p.m.

Pullman largely withdrew from the sleeping-car market but his dining-cars, which were mostly attached to existing trains – such as the *Brighton Belle* and the *Golden Arrow*, which ran between London and Paris via a ferry – became a byword for luxury.

It was the dawn of a golden age. The railway had become an essential part of the infrastructure of all the world's developed countries and, to a large extent, had a monopoly for many of its uses. There was simply no more efficient way for people, goods or minerals to be transported. And, by and large, it was about to get even better.

The Golden Arrow or *Flèche d'or* was a luxury boat train service between London and Paris which ran from 1926 to 1972 and at its fastest covered the journey in just six hours.

# A Sort of Golden Age

Railway nostalgics cling to the memory of a 'golden age' when journeys could be undertaken on comfortable trains with attentive service in luxurious surroundings. This myth is perpetuated by film depictions of journeys in the past, in which homely and brightly polished engines, belching out steam, whisk passengers to their destinations in pleasant, cosy compartments. Having been taken to their seats by deferential porters in smart uniforms, they might enjoy dinner *en route* served on white tablecloths. All the while, their train travels at a perfect pace, slow enough to allow them to enjoy the countryside, but fast enough to get them to their destination on time.

It is important to retain an element of scepticism about this image. Certainly the period between the turn of the century and the outbreak of the First World War was a very good time for the railways, and improvements to the trains and the standard of comfort continued to be made right up to the start of the Second World War. But even these supposedly halcyon days of railway travel were by no means perfect, especially for less affluent passengers or for those who happened to be travelling on remoter parts of the network, away from the main lines.

Many of the world's railways reached their apogee in terms of track miles around the time of the First World War, although several large countries, notably China, Japan and India, which had joined the railway age rather late, kept on building lines long afterwards. In the UK, rather neatly in chronological terms, the last major main line, the Great Central, which linked the new London station of Marylebone with the midlands and northwest, was completed in the final year of the 1800s and no new main lines were built until the opening of the high-speed Channel Tunnel Rail Link in the early twenty-first century. The Great Central was the brainchild of Sir Edward Watkin, one of those railway entrepreneurs with his fingers in so many pies that one wonders how he ever kept abreast of all his multifarious business dealings.

Variously described as a megalomaniac* and a gambler, he also ran the Metropolitan Railway and consequently built parts of what is now called the Circle Line of the London Underground. The Great Central, which fell victim to the Beeching closures of the 1960s – a terribly shortsighted move – went to Leicester and Nottingham, and then joined up with Watkin's Manchester, Sheffield & Lincolnshire Railway. Because the new railway duplicated many other routes, its unique selling point was to be a superior service whose mission statement was 'Rapid travel in luxury', with comfortable seats, elaborate furnishings and all-corridor trains that made the buffet accessible to both classes of passenger (which, oddly, were called first and third as second had been abolished).

Marylebone station, which opened in 1899, was the last of the London termini to be built, and was a modest affair compared with its three far grander neighbours a couple of miles to the east along the Euston Road. It was described rather cuttingly by the poet John Betjeman, a railway enthusiast and early campaigner for preservation of the railway heritage, as rather like 'a branch public library in a Manchester suburb'.[1]

By the turn of the century, the British rail system was virtually complete. Every town and most villages were connected through a network that stretched to 18,700 miles (30,094.7 km) and while another 1,000 miles (1,609.3 km) or so were added up to the start of the First World War, these were mostly connections between existing lines, short cuts between nearby towns and some suburban services, notably in London. With no need to devote all their surplus cash to further expansions, the railways were able, at last, to invest considerable resources into enhancing their

---

* Among Watkin's ventures were Wembley Tower, a proposed London equivalent to the Eiffel Tower, but it only reached the first level before being abandoned, and an attempt to dig a Channel tunnel, which was aborted after 1.8 miles (3 km) had been excavated.

services. Conditions for travellers had improved immeasurably in the last quarter of the nineteenth century. Services were more regular, carriages were cleaner and more comfortable, with the introduction of such facilities as heating, better lighting – gas and later electric – and, as mentioned in the previous chapter, toilets.

While the vast majority of passengers travelled in third or second class – though, as with Great Central, some lines only had two classes – the railway companies concentrated their efforts on the better-heeled traveller, and there was considerable competition to attract them with a better or faster service. For example, the Great Western ran services from London to Birkenhead with a ferry connection across the Mersey, to compete with the Liverpool services of the London & North Western, while Exeter could be reached by both the Southern and Great Western railways. The London & North Western even introduced a typing service on some of its trains for busy businessmen who had not brought their own secretaries with them, but apparently this was not widely used because of fears of industrial espionage.

Luxury became a key selling point. The London, Brighton & South Coast Railway launched a Pullman service to Brighton with seven smart Pullman cars which, its publicity claimed, were 'exquisitely upholstered, lighted by electricity, comfortably warmed and ventilated and fitted with all the latest improvements'. All that for just an hour's journey! The US also experienced a boom for premium travel in the early years of the twentieth century. Pullman's luxury train services flourished, increasing passenger numbers fivefold from a mere 5 million in 1900 to 26 million in 1914 despite the high supplementary fare. But American passengers on routine services also enjoyed a much better ride. During the early years of the twentieth century, electric lighting became standard and more trains were heated with steam, a much safer method than the dangerous coal-burning pot-belly stoves that had been the norm until then.

Between the wars, the Southern Railway undertook a programme to electrify nearly all of its tracks, which greatly increased efficiency and attracted vast numbers of extra passengers, particularly for its suburban network.

# ELECTRIFICATION!

700 MILES OF SOUTHERN RAIL-
WAY WILL BE ELECTRIFIED BY
SPRING NEXT YEAR ~ 3 NEW
SECTIONS OPEN THIS SUMMER
~ 3 ELECTRIC FOR EVERY STEAM
TRAIN NOW RUNNING ~ ~ ~
~ TOTAL COST £8,000,000

## WORLD'S GREATEST SUBURBAN ELECTRIC

# SOUTHERN

Technological improvements to the railways continued apace and the increasing profitability of the railway companies enabled their swift introduction. The speeding-up of services was seen not merely as a way of shortening journey times but also of attracting publicity. There had been huge public interest in a series of races from London to Scotland in 1888, and again in the 1890s, between the Great Northern Railway and its partner on the East Coast Main Line and the London & North Western Railway and its partner on the West Coast Main Line. Trains on the West Coast Main Line had been taking more than ten hours to reach Glasgow, an hour longer than those on the East Coast Main Line via Edinburgh, and consequently the Great Northern was winning over much of its rivals' business. Starting in June 1888, the companies made a series of tit-for-tat reductions in journey times, before holding a conference that August at which they agreed on a new timetable that was broadly two hours quicker than the old one. However, hostilities broke out again following the completion of the Forth bridge in December 1889, which enabled the companies to reach Aberdeen much more quickly than before.

In the summer of 1895, the companies competed over the lucrative 'grouse traffic', the aristocrats who hastened up to the Highlands for the annual shooting season that starts on 12 August. Both companies played dirty, running special services with few carriages and short stops at stations in order to achieve the shortest time. It was the London & North Western that triumphed, posting a time of 8 hours 32 minutes from London to Aberdeen at an average speed of 63 mph (101 km/h). Given that today's fastest service from London to the granite city – after more than a century of technological progress – takes only ninety minutes longer, this was a remarkable achievement.

In the aftermath of this 'Race to the North', many other companies followed suit by improving their timings and cutting out unnecessary delays. The search for speed, however, engendered something of a gung-ho spirit in some drivers, who were wont to open up their regulators a bit too easily. Such an attitude undoubtedly contributed to a disaster a year after the infamous August 1895 races to Aberdeen, when a train derailed at Preston on 15 August. The train was, unusually, not scheduled to stop there, and the drivers, ignoring the speed restriction on a curve of 10 mph (16 km/h), sped through at 45 mph (72 km/h), which inevitably caused the leading engine to career off the rails. Amazingly only one passenger was killed, but the accident led to the adoption of a more cautious attitude, and many express schedules were, as a result, made slacker. Indeed, such was the concern among the railway companies about the risk of accidents from overspeeding that in May 1904 when the Great Western's *City of Truro* was recorded, on a routine mail run from Plymouth to London, as travelling briefly at just above 100 mph (160 km/h), breaking the world record for a steam-powered locomotive, the company did not allow the feat to be publicized until three years later. Yet for all the GWR's caution, the *City of Truro*'s feat was a demonstration of the extent to which the technology of the railways had improved.

As well as being an era of technical advances, this was the period when the railway companies first looked to electrification as a viable alternative to steam. Electric trains have numerous benefits, not least in being far cleaner and having greater acceleration, but they require considerable investment in equipment, both on the tracks and for the locomotives. By the end of the 1880s, several electric-powered tram lines had begun operating after the inaugural line had started services in a suburb of Berlin in 1881. In the US, the first 'electric trolley' – as they were then called – ran in 1888 in Richmond, Virginia, and soon 'trolleycars' were appearing in numerous towns and cities across the country. They were more efficient and cheaper to operate than the horse-drawn tram systems that had operated in many places across the world since the middle of the nineteenth century.

The earliest electrified railway in Britain was also the world's first deep Tube line, the City & South London Railway (now part of the Northern Line), which began operating in 1890. Originally it had been envisaged as a cable railway, hauled by static steam engines, but as its 4-mile (6.5-km) length and numerous curves made this difficult, the availability of this new form of traction was a boon to its promoters. Even though the line was so underpowered in its early days that occasionally trains could not get up the slight incline to reach the terminus at King William Street in the city, and had to roll back for a second attempt, the railway was deemed a great success and other electric underground lines were soon being built in London and elsewhere. London's early lines, the Metropolitan and the District railways which now included numerous branches, were all electrified in the first decade of the twentieth century. Several short suburban services, such as the Liverpool Overhead railway and various suburban lines on the Lancashire & Yorkshire Railway followed suit, but Britain did not embark upon a large-scale programme of electrification until after the First World War.

It was Switzerland that became world leader in the use of electricity on the railways. The successful electrification in 1899 of the Burgdorf–Thun Railway made it Europe's first electrified main line. The Swiss realized quickly that electric traction was much more suitable than steam both for the numerous long tunnels being built on their rapidly expanding network and for their mountainous terrain, whose steep inclines electric locomotives would be more adept at tackling. Remarkably, in 1960 Switzerland proudly became the first country in the world to have a fully electrified network.

In 1895 the United States had become the first nation to electrify a main line when a new 4-mile (6.5-km) stretch of the Baltimore & Ohio Railroad was opened around Baltimore. However, apart from tunnels under the Hudson river connecting Manhattan with the mainland, by and large the US shunned electric power because of the cost of its introduction and to this day diesel locomotives provide power across virtually the whole network.

Given that electrification technology has been available for more than a century, and given its obvious advantages in terms of better performance and the lower maintenance costs of the locomotives, the conversion of railways to electric power has been slower than might have been expected. The high initial cost of conversion, the wide range of different technologies available – which led to incompatible systems being introduced within the same country – and the conservative nature of railway managements have all contributed to this rather sluggish rate of take-up. However, as we will see in the next chapter, the new lines, including the high-speed networks now proliferating across the world, are invariably electric-powered.

...

The US railway network peaked at over 250,000 miles (400,000 km) in 1916, during the First World War, making it by far the largest in the world. Today just under half of that network survives, principally for freight trains. The extent to which rail travel dominated the US before the advent of the motor car and its rapid spread after the First World War is demonstrated by the mushrooming of the interurban lines. These were in effect long-distance tram services, running between towns on very basic tracks usually by the side of a road. Their expansion was rapid once electric traction became widely available. A network of 2,000 miles (3,200 km) of these lines at the turn of the century had rocketed to a staggering 15,000 miles (24,150 km) by the outbreak of the First World War. By then, it would have been possible to travel all the way from New York to Wisconsin on a series of interurbans trundling between local towns. It would, too, have been a cheap ride as generally the fare was 10 cents for each interurban hop, a real bargain as they could be as long as 50 miles (80 km). Progress would have been slow, however, since these trains generally averaged little more than 20 mph (32 km/h), their primary purpose being to link rural and suburban areas with local towns, or to run between two nearby conurbations. In a pre-car age, interurbans were an efficient and cheap form of transport for local people, but they were a short-lived phenomenon. After the First World War, in the face of growing competition from motor vehicles, the interurban lines began to be closed. They would be all but wiped out in the 1930s when both vehicles and tracks needed renewing, which would not have been economically viable.

While the interurbans were electrically powered, diesel, rather than electricity, was widely seen as a better and cheaper way of modernizing the main lines. The introduction of diesel did not require major changes to the permanent way, apart from making it fit for higher-speed running by reducing curves and improving maintenance. Steam engines came to be seen as dirty and inefficient, and required constant maintenance. Thus, when the internal combustion engine was invented towards the end of the nineteenth century, attempts were made to harness this new form of power for the railways. The first trials used petrol but that proved inefficient – some small petrol engines were used in the First World War on the narrow-gauge lines that went right up to the trenches – and too expensive to be used for larger engines. However, the invention by Rudolf Diesel of his eponymous new form of internal combustion engine would have an enormous impact on railways across the world. Instead of a spark plug, the system relies on air heated by high compression to ignite the fuel. Various technical difficulties prevented the introduction of diesel locomotives until after the First World War but they then became the power mode of choice for modernizing railways and, in particular, for a new series of luxury trains. The pioneer was Germany, which began to experiment with diesel engines on its railways in the late 1920s. In 1932, the Reichsbahn introduced a revolutionary new diesel train, the *Fliegender Hamburger* ('Hamburg Flyer'), which ran between Berlin and Hamburg at an average speed of 76 mph (*c.* 122 km/h). This required it to cruise for long periods at 100 mph (160 km/h), faster than any other contemporary rail service across the world. Hitler would exploit such services for propaganda purposes as a demonstration of Germany's industrial strength and modernity.

Diesel technology was developed faster and more successfully in the United States than elsewhere. Aviation was regarded as limited and relatively dangerous; the railroad companies were quick to realize, however, that the car posed an existential threat, particularly to their passenger services, and responded by creating a new type of train, diesel-powered and streamlined, that was a step-change improvement from the laggardly and dirty steam engines. Consisting mainly of seven or eight coaches built of lightweight stainless steel and with newly developed alloys for the engines developed by General Electric, these trains provided a high level of personal comfort for the long journeys that the huge size of the country necessitated. They ran between major towns and cities, with limited stops to improve journey times, and were heavily promoted as the modern way to travel.

The first of these streamlined services, the aptly named *Pioneer Zephyr*, was launched in May 1934 with considerable fanfare by the Chicago, Burlington and Quincy Railroad (known as the Burlington), with an inaugural run covering the 1,000 miles (1,600 km) between Denver, Colorado and Chicago at an average speed of 78 mph (125 km/h). This was exceptionally fast, and required special measures such as patrol staff at all level-crossings. Nonetheless, a whole family of *Zephyrs* and *Limiteds*,

OVERLEAF In the 1930s, the US introduced a series of modern streamline trains like the Burlington *Zephyr*, which transformed train travel on the long distance journeys between east and west coasts.

so called because they called at few intermediate stations, sprang up, transforming long-distance travel on the American railroads.

Known as 'streamliners', these modern diesels were the pride of the railroad companies. They would later acquire enhancements such as observation cars and other amenities aimed at an affluent clientele. Their sleek designs, an eclectic mix of art deco and modernist features, would be imitated in other industries, notably by manufacturers of automobiles and domestic appliances. The railway operators competed with one another to provide the best food and the finest wines, often at subsidized rates in order to attract passengers onto the trains. The train service run by the Atchison, Topeka & Santa Fe Railway between Chicago, Illinois and Los Angeles, California – a two-day journey – often carried film stars and movie moguls on its flagship streamliner, the *Super Chief*. With its smooth ride, air-conditioned cars and general aura of luxury, it offered the best rail service in the world in the run-up to the Second World War. After the conflict ended, however, the streamliners soon succumbed to competition from aeroplanes and most of these services ceased operating, although some of the names have been retained by today's Amtrak trains.

In the US a couple of attempts were made to produce steam locomotives that could compete with the diesels. They turned out to be a failure, because diesel traction was not only faster and more reliable, but also, crucially, much cheaper over the long distances the trains had to travel. In Britain in the 1930s, however, there was a last-gasp attempt to see if steam locomotive technology could see off its rivals. The Great Western, for example, attempted to speed up services and boasted of having the fastest timetabled train service in the world, the *Cheltenham Flyer*, which ran to its Gloucestershire destination non-stop from Paddington at an average speed of 71 mph (114.3 km/h). The London–Scotland route, a lucrative rail market served by rival firms, the London, Midland & Scottish (LMS) on the west coast, and the London &

North Eastern Railway (LNER) on the east coast, was the scene of the most concerted attempts to speed up and improve services.

The timings between London and Scotland had not improved since the races of the 1890s described in the previous chapter and there was a gentleman's agreement between the two companies that no train should be timetabled to run between London and either of the two main Scottish cities in less than eight and a quarter hours. However, in 1932 this long-established agreement was torn up and, once again, a series of races took place. LNER's most famous train was the *Flying Scotsman* (not to be confused with the passenger express of that name that had operated on the East Coast Main Line between London and Edinburgh since 1862, with trains simultaneously leaving London King's Cross and Edinburgh Waverley stations at 10 a.m. each day). British steam trains of the 1920s and 30s not only went faster but also looked good, with streamlining that matched the art deco style characteristic of the interwar period. The much-admired designer of the *Flying Scotsman* was Nigel Gresley, chief mechanical engineer of the LNER, and his rivalry with William Stanier, his LMS counterpart, attracted widespread publicity as both companies conducted high-speed trials with new engines. Even the drivers became well known, and they were often asked for their autographs by passengers delighted by the rapidity of their journeys. Soon these new engines were easily exceeding the *City of Truro*'s record and regularly reached 90 mph (145 km/h). In a July 1938 test run in secret conditions on the East Coast Main Line under the guise of a brake test, Gresley's A4 Pacific, *Mallard*, achieved the remarkable speed of 126 mph (203 km/h), a record for steam engines that was never to be beaten.

The technological developments led to faster schedules. By 1938, the *Flying Scotsman* was timed to run between London and Edinburgh in just seven hours and the LMS's *Coronation Scot* between London and Glasgow in just six and a half. Arguably,

OVERLEAF The railway companies were proud of their scheme to modernize their networks, even publicizing highly technical devices such as this method of rapidly taking on coal.

however, the French engineer André Chapelon was the greatest locomotive designer of the age, and indeed quite possibly ever. Using scientific methods, rather than the usual engineer's trial-and-error process, he produced locomotives that were far more efficient – though even then only 12 per cent of the energy generated was used – which meant that they could perform as well as the diesel locomotives of the time. He was such a respected figure among engineers that a British locomotive was named after him, a rare honour.

For all their aesthetic splendour, the steam locomotives inevitably lost out to their electric and diesel rivals. However, even after the war, British Railways, nationalized in 1948, persisted with steam, producing a series of steam locomotives which, despite the joy they brought to trainspotters, were a retrograde step at a time when other countries were already focusing all their efforts on alternative forms of traction. The last British steam locomotive, *Evening Star*, entered service as late as 1960. This was also the year that the last steam engine ran on a main line in the US, although some would continue to survive on branch lines.

All the while, railway companies continued to make attempts to enhance the experience of train travel. Passengers were given free newspapers and magazines, and even offered, for a small fee, the loan of a headphone which could be plugged into a cable socket at the back of their seats to listen to the latest news and a selection of records chosen by an on-board DJ. Better dining facilities were provided and luggage could be taken to and from stations by special delivery services. These improvements were backed up by PR, which was largely invented and developed by the railways. Posters extolling the virtues of particular train trips had started appearing in the late nineteenth century, but started to be used widely in the Edwardian period. According to a history of the Great Western Railway – nicknamed 'God's Wonderful Railway': 'The GWR far outstripped its competitors with its excellent advertising. The company produced guidebooks in a good literary style, with clear, striking illustrations, all for three pence.'[2] Each year the company produced a booklet called *Holiday Haunts*, listing destinations that could easily be reached via its services. Other companies followed the GWR's lead and created their own publicity initiatives. The London & North Western produced a set of postcards, each of which showed one of its trains passing through a picturesque landscape, and sold millions of them through vending machines. Several companies produced booklets listing all the types of locomotive they used, although it was not really until after the Second World War that the hobby of trainspotting became a national pastime in Britain for adolescent boys.*

The experience of rail travel may have been rather mixed but the early decades of the twentieth century were definitely

_____
\* Including the author!

The *Flying Scotsman* locomotive, designed by Sir Nigel Gresley, was built in 1923 for the London and North Eastern Railway at Doncaster Works and has been preserved in working order.

the golden age of the railway poster. Many railway companies produced high-class publicity, employing the top artists of the day to create designs that endure today. London Undergound, under the guidance of its long-time managing director, Frank Pick, became synonymous with good design. The Underground not only produced literally hundreds of posters that adorn many living-rooms and bedrooms to this day, but created one of the world's first and most famous logos, the roundel, and an elegant sans serif typeface, Johnston, that still adorns every Tube sign.

The consolidation of the UK's railways into the 'Big Four' companies in 1923 enabled them to devote considerable effort to marketing and advertising. Posters were the mainstay of their publicity campaigns with acres of free wall space at stations available to be adorned with advertisements, both for the railways themselves and for other businesses. As well as helping to market seaside resorts and other tourist destinations, the railway companies' memorable posters featured the famous express trains described earlier in this chapter.

The interwar years were the closest to a golden age of rail that there ever would be. But, despite the modernization of the Victorian railway network, and the consolidation of railway companies, which brought about economies of scale, the railways were under siege during this period on both sides of the Atlantic. The networks of both Britain and the US were worked very hard during the Second World War, with little investment to compensate for their overuse. The lack of oil and resulting rationing of petrol during the conflict gave them a boost, as people had no alternative but to travel by train. The post-war period, however, would usher in decline for the railway industry, characterized by closures and cutbacks. The golden age of rail was well and truly over.

From the Edwardian era to the Second World War, Frank Pick, managing director of the London Underground, commissioning thousands of posters of the highest standard, which remain a fantastic legacy of this transport system.

# HOLIDAY ATTRACTIONS

*For The Zoo, Book To Regent's Park or Camden Town*

UNDERGROUND

# A Nineteenth-Century Invention for the Twenty-First Century

The immediate post-war period was cruel to the railways. Once the blanket of wartime austerity had been thrown off, the greater affluence of people, together with the renewed availability of cheap fuel, meant that for the first time car ownership became possible for the masses. The corollary was the neglect of the railway network and the beginning of widespread closures. Who needs railways when the shiny car outside your front door can take you directly to your destination at a fraction of the cost?

The Second World War had devastated many parts of the European railway network. In Britain, even though the damage had been lighter, the railways were in a parlous state because, as a key component of the war effort, they had been grossly overused. After the victory of the Labour party in the July 1945 election, following the end of the conflict in Europe, the railways in Britain were nationalized in 1948 as it was clear the private sector would be unable to afford the investment needed to bring them up to scratch. In the US, too, overuse of the railways meant they were slow to recover in the aftermath. Other countries, with war-wrecked networks, also nationalized their railways.

By the 1950s the railways in Europe had been patched up but they had not regained their pre-war pizzazz. Services were already starting to be run down in the face of competition from roads, which were receiving the lion's share of government investment in transport infrastructure. With train services declining and cars becoming commonplace, the move away from railways was remarkably swift. In West Germany, for instance, the newly created state-owned Deutsche Bahn went from having a 37.5 per cent share of the total passenger market in 1950 to just 7.8 per cent two decades later. There were similar, if less marked, declines in other European countries. Those behind the Iron Curtain, however, largely kept their railways intact as, by and large, citizens were unable to buy cars and trains therefore remained the cornerstone of the transport networks. (Ironically, it was only after the removal of the Iron Curtain in 1989 that the countries of Eastern Europe started to reduce their networks – at the very moment when their counterparts in the West were realizing that virtually every line of their neglected and underfunded network could be turned into a useful economic or social asset.)

Attempts were made in Western Europe to go against the grain of the post-war decline of the railways with the creation of the Trans-Europ Expresses (TEE) linking major cities. These were jointly operated by several state-owned railway companies as part of the initiative to create the Common Market, the precursor to the European Union. Half a dozen services, running for example between Paris and Amsterdam, and Frankfurt and Zurich, were launched in 1957 and the network quickly grew to encompass seventy-three cities. TEE trains managed to attract business travellers and flourished for a time, but aviation inevitably stole a major part of their custom and they began to be phased out in the 1970s.

In the US, the decline of the passenger network was even faster than in Europe. In the immediate post-war years, the prestige trains kept going and many streamliners were fitted with observation cars for the first time. However, within a few years – as flight became safer and a more extensive network of air routes was created, and most people with a job bought a car – rail travel numbers fell away sharply. While in 1930, 75 per cent of passenger traffic was by rail, this had fallen to just 7 per cent forty years later, and most of those trips were being made by commuters in the few cities, such as Chicago and New York, that had retained their suburban lines.

The speed with which passenger rail networks in the US were shut down was in part due to the American predilection for individual rather than collective solutions. Even though the railroads had been the cornerstone of the American transport system for several generations, once motor vehicles became

OVERLEAF The railways performed a vital transport function during the Second World War, but were left damaged by bombs, overused and underinvested, leading to their nationalization in 1948.

cheaply available, there was an unseemly rush to dispense with the railways, which had never quite overcome the bad reputation garnered in the days of the robber barons. As passengers deserted them and the companies found they could not extricate themselves from union agreements made in the good times, the railroads soon found themselves in a very weak financial position – especially when they lost the longstanding and lucrative contracts from the United States Post Office. However, they were reluctant to accept state subsidies or control, but instead moved to close down loss-making services as soon as possible to concentrate on freight. Indeed, such was the haste with which the railroad companies wanted to get out of the passenger business

The postwar era was a period of decline for many railways across the world, resulting in the abandonment of many lines, like this branch in Poland, photographed in 2015.

that on one occasion travellers were turfed off their train halfway through its journey as the company had just got permission from the Federal authorities to cease providing the service. By the 1960s, bankruptcies of railways with little freight business were becoming commonplace. Mergers kept a few of them afloat for a bit longer but, in 1970, all remaining US rail passenger services were handed over to Amtrak, a government-owned organization. The greatest free-enterprise country of the world had been forced to recognize that railways could not be profitable in the face of unfettered competition from the car and the plane. US rail freight, too, declined in the 1970s but was revived in the 1980s. Today it is a highly profitable business mainly in the hands of half a dozen huge companies.

In the US, about half the network was closed down in the post-war decades, with the rest surviving thanks to freight. In Britain, there had been a trickle of line closures from the 1930s but the process of shutting lines accelerated after the end of the Second World War. A massive series of closures swiftly followed the publication in 1963 of the seminal report by Richard Beeching, the head of British Railways, *The Reshaping of British Railways*, which was a euphemism for radically cutting back the network. Mostly this affected branch lines that were seen as uneconomic, but several key main lines were also shut, notably the Great Central and the Oxford–Cambridge line (which actually had not originally been slated for closure by Beeching). Beeching's report led to the closure of 4,000 miles (6,437 km) of railway over the next decade, one-quarter of the total, as well as 3,000 stations.

For a time in the 1960s and 1970s, when car ownership across the world was rising rapidly and little investment was going into the railways, it seemed as if the iron road might have had its day. However, towards the end of the twentieth century, as the motorways clogged up and many city centres became gridlocked, railway travel was able to reassert itself as a desirable form of transport in two main areas: long-distance intercity travel for both leisure and business passengers; and suburban journeys for commuters.

A few countries continued to build conventional railways in the post-war period, though they were very much the exception. For instance, the Baikal–Amur Mainline, which parallels the eastern part of the Trans-Siberian, was built by the Soviet government over a period of fifty years at a terrible human cost. It was finally completed in 1991, after the Communist regime had been overthrown. In India, the Konkan Railway between Mumbai and Goa in western India was opened as late as 1998, and Indian Railways is building other new lines into remote areas.

The turning point for long-distance train travel was technological development. In Japan, an excellent market for trains since most people live in the densely populated lowland areas, overcrowding had become a perennial problem on the 320-mile (515-km) line between Tokyo and Osaka. Rather than doubling the track on the old line, Japanese National Railways, which was state-owned at the time, decided to build an entirely new route, uncluttered by the freight and local services that slowed down the existing one. Deciding to construct the line was a brave move by the railway company as the conventional wisdom of the time was that railways were redundant and would be overtaken by cars and planes. However, it proved to be a far-sighted decision: within a generation the concept would be copied around the world, helping to ensure that the railways remained relevant in the twenty-first century. The inspiration behind the Tokyo–Osaka line was not only the overcrowding on the existing railway route but also the allocation of the 1964 summer Olympics to Japan which, still recovering from the ravages of the Second World War, required major improvements in its transport infrastructure. Construction took just under five years and the project was completed just in time for the opening ceremony of the Tokyo Olympics. Dubbed 'Shinkansen', which literally means 'new trunk line', the pioneering new railway, popularly known as the 'bullet train', established the template for future high-speed line projects with its dedicated tracks, electric traction, lack of sharp curves and steep elevations, and in-cab signalling. The trains operated at 125 mph (200 km/h) – rather slow compared with today's high-speed lines across the world, which routinely run at 186 mph (299 km/h), but this still allowed the journey between the two cities to be reduced by half to just three hours and ten minutes. While the new lines experienced few technical mishaps, passengers suffered pain in their ears and, embarrassingly, splashes from the toilets because of the increase in air pressure when the trains entered the numerous lengthy tunnels. As a result, the train compartments had to be pressurized, an expensive and complex task, but one that solved both the problems of earache and misbehaving toilets.

A decade and a half would elapse before any other country followed suit. The French already held the railway world speed record, having run an electric train at 206 mph (331.5 km/h) in 1955, but in that attempt the track had buckled, demonstrating that high-speed routes were best kept separate from conventional services. Again, it was overcrowding, in this case on the Paris–Lyons line, that instigated the building of a new high-speed line. The Sud-Est Ligne à Grande Vitesse, the first high-speed line in Europe, opened between the two cities in 1981, having taken seven years to build. The Train à Grande Vitesse (TGV) was, like the Shinkansen, an instant success, all but wiping out the frequent air service on the route. Soon other TGV lines were being built and the French high-speed network now radiates from Paris to all points of France's *Hexagone*. The services include the world's longest non-stop train service, the near 500-mile (800-km) route between Paris and Marseille, a journey that takes a mere three hours.

OVERLEAF High-speed trains, introduced in Japan, have spearheaded a railway renaissance. This photograph from 2012 shows how the Shinkansen has evolved, the newer trains on the right contrasting with an earlier version.

The successes in both France and Japan ensured high-speed rail soon caught on elsewhere, and across the world other countries soon developed their own versions. In Europe, Spain embarked on an ambitious programme to link every major town and city by high-speed rail and by the early 2010s had developed the continent's biggest network, overtaking France. Italy has completed a line that runs through the spine of the country and, unusually, has two rival operating services: the Frecciarossa trains run by the state-owned rail company and Italo trains provided by a private concern, Nuovo Trasporto Viaggiatori. In Germany, a rather different concept developed, with high-speed sections linking parts of the conventional track.

In Britain, the only high-speed railway is the 67-mile (108-km) line between London and the entrance to the Channel Tunnel used by the Eurostar services linking London St Pancras with Brussels, Paris and a few other destinations, although construction has started on HS2, a line from the capital to Birmingham but which is eventually planned to reach Leeds and Manchester. In the US, despite the purchase of high-speed rolling stock for use along the northeast corridor, the lack of dedicated track and the retention of level-crossings has meant that services along this heavily used route remain slow by international standards. A plan to build a high-speed line linking San Francisco with Los Angeles has stalled following huge cost increases. Elsewhere, high-speed trains are spreading across the world with schemes either open or under construction in South Korea, Taiwan, Morocco, Turkey, the Ukraine and Saudi Arabia. China is by some distance the world leader, devoting huge resources to creating a massive network that encompasses two-thirds of all high-speed lines in the world and which reached 25,000 miles (40,000 km) in 2022, and is expected to rise further by 2030.

The growth in metro systems has been just as remarkable, not least in China itself where from a total of just five systems at the turn of the century, by 2019 there were thirty-five cities with underground lines. The city with the largest network is Shanghai, which has a staggering 420 miles (675 km) on sixteen lines – contrast that with the world's oldest system, the London Underground, which has just 250 miles (400 km) on eleven lines. There are currently around 200 metro systems in towns and cities across the world, but many more are expected to open in the next decade. Trams, which were wiped out in many countries and scaled back in most others in the post-war period, have also enjoyed a remarkable renaissance and new tracks are opening virtually every month across the world. While some of these are in towns and cities that previously never had a tramway, ironically most are in places where lines were closed in the post-war period, when trams were seen as unwieldy inconveniences that got in the way of cars and vans in urban areas.

The growth in both tram and underground systems is not only proof that past transport policies of closing them down or avoiding new investment were both mistaken and shortsighted, but also belated acceptance of the harsh reality that cars in urban centres cannot be the focus of transport networks. Even in the US, where rail use has tailed off so sharply, the idea of 'transit-oriented development', in which residents have easy access to railways or trams, thereby obviating the need to use cars, has become popular.

Similarly, for longer-distance routes, overcrowding on major motorways and the speed advantage of trains, even conventional ones, mean that intercity rail services remain an attractive alternative to the car. And given the downsides of air travel – notably its intense security processes and the need to access airports that are located out of town – rail travel also compares favourably with the aeroplane. Freight, too, where rail is competitive for longer distances, has thrived in particular sectors of industry, such as minerals and aggregates, and in large countries, notably the US,

Russia and India. Furthermore, the environmental advantages of train travel in a gradually warming world are now part of an impetus that favours investment in rail.

Another widely recognized advantage of rail is safety. While major rail accidents were commonplace in the nineteenth and twentieth centuries, they are now a rarity. Many countries go several years without a fatal crash on their networks. For example, there have only been two accidents involving the death of train passengers since 2002 on the British Rail network –February 2007 when a Virgin train derailment killed one person at Grayrigg in Cumbria and another derailment at Stonehaven in Aberdeenshire in August 2020 which resulted in three fatalities. This improvement has been achieved through studying the causes of accidents to learn the lessons from them and by the widespread use of enhanced technology. This is in sharp contrast to the roads, where death tolls are still remarkably high even though they have declined in recent years. While the Covid pandemic resulted in passenger numbers being reduced to levels not seen before the railway age, the recovery has been, for the most part, relatively fast though patterns of usage have changed with more leisure travellers and fewer commuters. The railways have managed to overcome yet another challenge.

...

The railways will never again have the ubiquitous role they enjoyed in the pre-motor vehicle era, when they were effectively the only way to get about for trips longer than a few miles. The days of travelling to the next village or town on a rickety branch line served by a couple of trains daily in a train that probably had a few freight wagons tacked on the back have disappeared, like the steam locomotive, forever. We should not be nostalgic but nor should we forget the ways in which the railways helped create the civilization we live in today. Their influence is permanent and incredibly profound, as this book demonstrates. The joy is that in the twenty-first century we are still able to enjoy the advantages of train travel, whether it is for our daily commute (which may take place on overcrowded trains, but would be far worse if the railways did not exist), or for long journeys during which the constantly changing view from the train window makes up for the fact that our electronic devices may not always work on the move. We should celebrate the fact that the railway pioneers, from the Stephensons onwards, would recognize today's railways as the descendants of their invention, even if the modern train bears little resemblance to the *Rocket*. The railways, having survived a period of decline, are now an established part of modern life and will be for generations to come. That is not something that can be said about many nineteenth-century inventions.

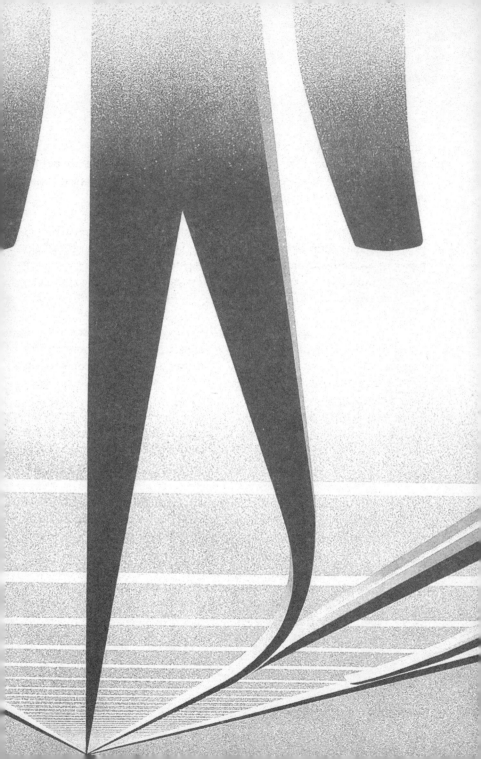

# Timeline

1000 BC
Greeks use a system of tracks on roads to enable smoother passage of carts.

14th–15th century
Tracks are used for carts in mines, initially in Germany but later in England.

1604
Britain's first wagonway is built by Huntingdon Beaumont at a mine in Wollaton, Nottinghamshire.

1725
Opening of the 5-mile (8-km) long Tanfield Wagonway, which includes the world's first large masonry railway bridge, the Causey Arch.

1774
James Watt produces the first stationary steam engine.

1799
Richard Trevithick devises a high-pressure steam engine and two years later builds a full-size steam road locomotive.

1803
The first public railway, the Surrey Iron Railway, a double-tracked plateway, opens, linking the towns of Wandsworth and Croydon. It was a double-track plateway throughout with a gauge of about 5 feet (1.5 m).

1807
The first fare-paying service opens on the Oystermouth Railway in Swansea, south Wales, with horse-drawn carriages.

1808
Richard Trevithick runs a circular steam railway with locomotive *Catch Me Who Can* near the present site of Euston station in London.

**1814**
George Stephenson constructs his first locomotive, *Blücher*, for the Killingworth wagonway.

**1825**
The Stockton & Darlington Railway opens, its route devised by George Stephenson, who also produced its first locomotive, *Locomotion*, but most trains are horse-drawn.

**1830**
*May*: In the US, the first steam-operated railway, the Baltimore & Ohio Railroad, opens its first 13 miles (21 km) of track.
*July*: The first French railway, part of the Saint-Étienne–Lyons railway, opens.
*September*: The Liverpool & Manchester Railway starts operating the world's first double-tracked, all-steam-powered railway linking two major conurbations.

**1835**
*May*: The first Belgian railway opens between Brussels and Mechelen.

**1837**
Main lines open for the first time in Germany, Austria, Russia and France.

**1842**
*May*: The world's first major rail disaster occurs in Versailles, near Paris, when a train derails, causing at least 50 deaths.

**1843**
The first international rail line, connecting Brussels with Cologne, opens.

**1853**
Railways introduced to India, with a train running from Bombay (now Mumbai) to Thane.

**1854**
The first section of the inaugural African railway is completed in Alexandria, Egypt.

**1863**
*January*: The world's first underground line, the 4-mile (6.5-km) long Metropolitan Railway in London, opens, using steam engines with condensers.

1869
The first transcontinental line across America is completed, running from Omaha, Nebraska, to Sacramento, California.

1881
The world's first electric tram line begins running in Lichterfelde, near Berlin, Germany.

1889
The Armagh train disaster in Northern Ireland leads to widespread introduction of safety measures across the UK.

1890
The first electric underground railway, the City & South London, opens.

1904
The world's longest railway, the Trans-Siberian, opens fully between Moscow and Vladivostok when a section around Lake Baikal connects the two halves. In the UK, *City of Truro*, a Great Western locomotive, becomes the first steam engine to exceed 100 mph (161 km/h).

1913
Diesel-powered locomotives start being used in Sweden.

1915–17
Three of the world's worst ever accidents occur during the First World War, all carrying troops: Quintinshill in Scotland in May 1915 (226 deaths), Ciurea in Romania in January 1917 (up to 1,000 deaths) and St Michel de Maurienne in December 1917 (at least 650 deaths).

1923
Consolidation of UK railways into four large regionally based companies: the London & North Western, the London Midland & Scottish, the Great Western and the Southern.

1938
The streamlined steam engine *Mallard* runs at a record speed of 126 mph (203 km/h) between Peterborough and Grantham in the midlands.

1948
Britain's railways are nationalized.

**1961**
The last main line steam engine runs in the US.

**1964**
The world's first high-speed train, operating between Tokyo and Osaka, is introduced in time for that year's Olympics.

**1968**
Last steam train run by British Rail.

**1971**
Amtrak, owned by the federal government, takes over most passenger rail services in the US to prevent further closures.

**1981**
The first European high-speed train line begins operating in France between Paris and Lyon.

**1994**
The Channel Tunnel, which establishes a rail link between Britain and mainland Europe, opens.

**1997**
Re-privatization of Britain's railways is completed.

**2003**
*September*: Britain's first section of high-speed line opens.

**2008**
China's first high-speed line opens between Beijing and Tianjin. By 2019 there are 18,000 miles (29,000 km) of track in operation, and it is expected that this will rise to 24,000 miles (38,500 km) by 2025.

**2022**
Britain's most expensive railway, the £18.8 billion Elizabeth Line, opens.

# Select bibliography

There are literally thousands of books written on the railways, with more than 25,000 listed in George Ottley's *Bibliography of British Railway History* alone, and any bibliography is bound to be partial. There are more than 1,000 in my own personal library. So I have limited myself to two or three suggestions on each area. I have listed several of my own books, which are social histories aimed very much at the general reader. By and large, I have avoided tomes that concentrate on technology as they are mostly of interest to the specialist and it is not an area on which I tend to focus.

World Railways

Covering the world's railways in a single volume is an impossible task. My book *Blood, Iron & Gold* (Atlantic Books, 2009) gives a big-picture outline focusing in particular on the great transcontinental lines. I also wrote a book for Dorling Kindersley, *The Iron Road* (2014), which covers a variety of specific subjects in forty-three chapters. There are numerous coffee table-type books, with lots of illustrations, but many are out of date as these books have rather gone out of fashion. The best examples include: O. S. Nock's *World Atlas of Railways* (Mitchell Beazley, 1978); Nicholas Faith's *Locomotion* (BBC Books, 1993); and *Two Centuries on the Rails* (Aurum, 2004) by Anthony Burton. Nicholas Faith's *The World the Railways Made* (Bodley Head, 1990; reissued by Head of Zeus, 2018) was pioneering in that it concentrated on the social impact rather than the technology.

## Britain's Railways

My book *Fire and Steam* (Atlantic Books, 2007) is a general history of Britain's railways (with a lengthy bibliography). Professor Jack Simmons produced a series of excellent histories of the railways covering their social and economic impact, notably *The Railways of Britain* (1986). *The Oxford Companion to British Railway History* is a useful if rather pedantic encyclopedia, but undoubtedly the best and most comprehensive volume is Simon Bradley's rather clumsily titled *The Railways: Nation, Network and People* (Profile Books, 2015), which covers every aspect of the railways' impact on British history.

## US Railroads

My book *The Great Railway Revolution* (Atlantic Books, 2012) was the first general history for some time. Earlier ones include Albro Martin's optimistic *Railroads Triumphant* (Oxford University Press, 1992) and Stewart H. Holbrook's idiosyncratic *The Story of American Railroads* (Bonanza Books, 1947). There are numerous books on the story of the Transcontinental, which has mythical status among many railway folk, the best of which is David Haward Bain's *Empire Express* (Viking Penguin, 1999). Dee Brown's *Hear That Lonesome Whistle Blow* is an account of how the railroads conquered the West and lives up to its wonderfully evocative title. One of the best social history books ever written on the railroads is Theodore Kornweibel Jr's *Railroads in the African American Experience: A Photographic Journey* (Johns Hopkins University Press, 2010), which is a superbly written and wonderfully illustrated little-told story of the railroads' mistreatment of their black workers.

## Underground Railways and Trams

My *The Subterranean Railway* (Atlantic Books, 2nd edition, 2012) is a history of the London Underground, which has a rich literature. The standard work which covers all forms of London transport is the two-volume *A History of London Transport* (George Allen & Unwin, 1963 and 1974) by T. C. Barker and Michael Robbins. There are histories of every line published by Capital Transport and written by various authors. Two other books by Capital Transport are enormously informative: *Transit Maps of the World* (Capital Transport, 2003; updated Penguin, 2015) by Mark Ovenden covers every system in the world, showing the widespread influence of the original London Underground map by Harry Beck, and Tim Demuth's *The Spread of London Underground* (Capital Transport, 2003) illustrates its development with maps of every decade. On trams in the UK, the best book is *Rails in the Road: A History of Tramways in Britain and Ireland* (Pen & Sword, 2016), which has fantastic evocative photographs and illustrations of the tram era and includes the modern revival. *The Electric Interurban Railways in America* (Stanford University Press, 1960) is an academic book by George W. Hilton and John F. Due on the amazing and largely forgotten story of the interurbans, which at one time ran alongside almost every major highway in the US.

## Other Railways

Apart from my books on the Trans-Siberian (*To the Edge of the World*; Atlantic Books, 2013) and on Indian railways (*Railways and the Raj*; Atlantic Books, 2017) I will just list a few books chosen because they are particularly good, rather than because of their subject matter. Oddly, for example, the Dutch railways are blessed with a particularly good and well-illustrated history, *Railways in the Netherlands: A Brief History 1834–1994* by Arthur J. Veenendaal Jr (Stanford University Press, 2001). Similarly, one of the best social histories of an individual country's railways is Neill Atkinson's *Trainland: How Railways Made New Zealand* (Random House, 2007), which, again, is well illustrated and puts the railway in context as a key part of the young nation's history. Unusually, Australia's best railway history was written by a woman, a rare breed in railway literature, Patsy Adam Smith – *Romance of Australian Railways* (Rigby, 1973). George Tabor's *The Cape to Cairo Railway & River Routes* (Genta, 2003) is a rare good book on African railways, covering Cecil Rhodes' vain attempt to run a railway across the whole continent. I generally don't like coffee table books that focus on pictures but those in *China: The World's Last Steam Railway: A Photographic Essay* by John Tickner, Gordon Edgar and Adrian Freeman are just astonishing and show a lot of the country beyond its railways.

## Other Books of Interest

Again, just a handful of books that stick out from the pack. *Railwaywomen: Exploitation, Betrayal and Triumph in the Workplace* (Hastings Press, 2005) by Helena Wojtczak is the first to look at a totally neglected area, the role and the mistreatment of women in the railways. *Dow's Dictionary of Railway Quotations* (Johns Hopkins University Press, 2006) by Andrew Dow is precisely what its title implies, and a wonderful compilation. Michael Williams has written a series of books about obscure branch lines, the first of which is *On the Slow Train: Twelve Great British Railway Journeys* (Preface Publishing, 2010). The great writer Matthew Engel's book *Eleven Minutes Late* (Macmillan, 2009), a train journey to the soul of Britain, is an attempt to discover why we love trains despite all their failings. Michael Freeman also looks at the way railways have caught the public's interest in his *Railways and the Victorian Imagination* (Yale University Press, 1999). And lastly, a mention of my personal favourite among my own books: *Engines of War* (Atlantic Books, 2012), which covers the way that railways created a different – bloodier and longer – form of warfare. I could go on …

# Notes

Why Railways?

1  Hylton, S., *The Grand Experiment: The Birth of the Railway Age 1820–1845* (Ian Allan, 2007), p. 11.

1:  The Idea Takes Root

1  Ferneyhough, F., *Liverpool and Manchester Railway, 1830–1980* (Book Club Associates, 1980), p. 13.

2  Ibid. p 13.

3  Davies, H., *George Stephenson, The Remarkable Life of the Founder of the Railways* (Weidenfeld and Nicolson, 1975), p. 124.

4  Letter from George Stephenson to Edward Pease, quoted in Ferneyhough, F., *Liverpool and Manchester Railway, 1830–1980* (Book Club Associates, 1980), p. 17.

5  Ferneyhough, F., *Liverpool and Manchester Railway, 1830–1980* (Book Club Associates, 1980), pp. 28–9.

6  Smiles, S., *The Life of George Stephenson* ([1881] The University Press of the Pacific, 2001), p. 108.

7  Davies, H., *George Stephenson, The Remarkable Life of the Founder of the Railways* (Weidenfeld and Nicolson, 1975), p. 152.

8  Widely quoted and taken from a longer quote in Garfield, S., *The Last Journey of William Huskisson* (Faber and Faber, 2002), p. 20.

9  Holbrook, S. H., *The Story of American Railroads* (Bonanza Books, 1947), p. 23.

2:  Railways Everywhere

1  Holbrook, S. H., *The Story of American Railroads* (Bonanza Books, 1947), p. 40.

2  Ward, J. A., *Railroads and the Character of America, 1820–1887* (University of Tennessee Press, 1986), p. 28.

3  Douglas, G. H., *All Aboard: The Railroad in American Life* (Paragon House, 1992), p. 37.

4  Kornweibel, Jr, T., *Railroads in the African American Experience: A Photographic Journey* (Johns Hopkins University Press, 2010), p. 11.

5  Lewin, H. G., *The Railway Mania and its Aftermath 1845–1852* ([1936] David & Charles, 1968), p. 121.

3:   Changing the World

1   Quoted in Simmons, J., *The Railway in Town and Country, 1830–1914* (David & Charles, 1986), p. 61.

2   Mayhew, H., *The Shops and Companies of London and the Trades and Manufacturers of Great Britain* (Strand, 1865), p. 146.

3   Douglas, G. H., *All Aboard: The Railroad in American Life* (Paragon House, 1992), p. 232.

4   Holbrook, S. H., *The Story of American Railroads* (Bonanza Books, 1947), p. 60.

5   Williams, F. S., *Our Iron Roads: Their History, Construction and Social Influences* (Bemrose, 1852), p. 285.

6   Bradley, S., *The Railways: Nation, Network and People* (Profile Books, 2015), p. 90.

7   Ibid. p. 92.

8   Middleton, W. D., Smerk, G. M. and Diehl, R. L., *Encyclopedia of North American Railroads* (Indiana University Press, 2007), p. 244.

4:   Nationbuilding

1   Pirenne, H., *L'Histoire de Belgique, 1862–1935*, author's trans., (Hardpress Publishing, 2013), p. 64.

2   Ashley, S. A., *Making Liberalism Work: The Italian Experience, 1860–1914* (Greenwood Publishing, 2003), p. 40.

3   Quoted in Mitchell, A., *The Great Train Race: Railways and the Franco-German Rivalry* (Berghahn Books, 2000), p. 63.

4   Quoted in Weber, T., *The Northern Railroads in the Civil War, 1861–1865* ([1952] Indiana University Press, 1995), p. 141.

5:   Robber Barons and Railway Cathedrals

1   Richards, J., in Wheeler, J. (ed.), *Ruskin and Environment: The Storm-Cloud of the Nineteenth Century* (Manchester University Press, 1995), p. 124.

2   Harter, J., *World Railways of the Nineteenth Century: A Pictorial History in Victorian Engravings*, p 275.

6:   A Safer and Better Journey

1   Middleton, W. D., Smerk, G. M. and Diehl, R. L., *Encyclopedia of North American Railroads* (Indiana University Press, 2007), p. 39.

2   Ibid. p. 90.

3   Rolt, L. T. C., *Red for Danger* (David and Charles, 4th edition, 1982), p. 163.

4   Bradley, S., *The Railways: Nation, Network and People* (Profile Books, 2015), p. 50.

7:   A Sort of Golden Age

1   Betjeman, J., *London's Historic Railway Stations* (John Murray, 1972), p. 117.

2   Maggs, C., *A History of the Great Western Railway* (Amberley Publishing, 2013), p. 173.

# Index